# AMERICAN GIBRALTAR

# AMERICAN GIBRALTAR
## MONTAUK AND THE WARS OF AMERICA

# HENRY OSMERS

**Outskirts Press, Inc.**
**Denver, Colorado**

# Contents

# List of Illustrations

# Acknowledgements

I AM EXTREMELY grateful to the following people for their assistance with this project. First, a special thanks to Dick White, member of the board of directors of the Montauk Historical Society and the Lighthouse Committee for the Montauk Point Lighthouse, for the suggestion of the topic for this book. Thanks to Society president Betsy White for graciously allowing access to documents and photos. Trisha Wood and Brian Pope of the Montauk Point Lighthouse Museum offered advice and encouragement.

Several librarians were extremely helpful with my work, in particular Gina Piastuck and Steve Boerner of the Long Island Collection at the East Hampton Library, who were enthusiastic in their assistance. Time spent with Robin Strong of the Montauk Library is always enlightening and enriching. Mark Rothenberg in the Local History Room of the Patchogue-Medford Library offered great advice and good conversation. John Hyslop and Erik Huber of the Long Island Division of the Queensboro Public Library in Jamaica, New York, assisted in providing the Eugene Armbruster photos.

Away from Long Island, thanks to Wallace Dailey, curator of the Theodore Roosevelt Collection at the Houghton Library, Harvard University, for the photos of Colonel Roosevelt and Camp Wikoff.

What really made the manuscript come alive were interviews with several Montauk residents who lived through the military experience at Montauk. Fred Houseknecht spoke of his time at Camp Hero immediately following World War II. James (Jim) T. Sullivan, in a recorded interview with the Montauk Library in 2003, spoke of the year he was stationed at Camp Hero in the late 1950s. Interesting stories of Montauk during World War II and the Cold War era were shared with the writer by Frank (Shank) Dickinson, John Ecker, Vinnie Grimes, Frank Tuma, Dave Webb, and Dick White.

Men from other parts of the country that served at Montauk were also gracious in sharing their remembrances: Winfred Gronley, Byron Lindsey, and Bruce McAuliffe. Philip Lewis recalled his youth at the Montauk Point Lighthouse in the late 1950s when his father Ira was stationed there with the Coast Guard. All of these people made my journey through Montauk's military history a wonderful experience.

# Dedication

*In memory of Dr. Myron H. Luke (1906-2000),
whose passion for Long Island history inspired my own.*

# Introduction

ON LONG ISLAND before the American Revolution, settlers were aware of occasional Indian wars, especially those that took place on the East End on Montauk. Although the Montaukett Indians built their own fortifications, the threat of war from Indian tribes from Connecticut and Rhode Island persisted in the mid 1600s, occasionally erupting in battles on Long Island soil, and lasting until the late 1650s. The Montauk Peninsula, settled in 1660, was destined in the next 260 years to become pastureland for the cattle, sheep, goats, and horses for the communities of East Hampton, Amagansett, and points further west.

Deemed unfit for settlement, only four structures existed on the nearly 11,000 acres of Montauk from the mid 1700s until the early 1880s. First House, built 1744 and rebuilt 1798 (burned 1909), stood within the boundaries of present Hither Hills State Park just off the Old Montauk Highway. Second House, built 1746 and rebuilt 1797, still stands on Montauk Highway at the western edge of Montauk village. Third House, built 1747 and rebuilt 1806, stands on a rise north of present Montauk Point State Parkway about two miles from the lighthouse. The early inhabitants of these houses were "keepers" of a sort, tending to the organization and paperwork involved in maintaining the thousands of animals that grazed across the hills and valleys of Montauk.

The fourth "house" was the Montauk Point Lighthouse. Built atop Turtle Hill at Montauk Point in 1796 by New York architect and bricklayer John McComb (1763-1853) in response to complaints about numerous shipping mishaps and disasters along the shores of the East End, it continues to guide vessels today.

Given these circumstances, it seemed that Montauk was destined to be forever peaceful and simple, though the occasional ship might still run ashore, albeit less frequently since the lighthouse was constructed.

Since 1775 when Americans began their battle for independence, Long Island has been perceived by military leaders as a location significant to the defense of our country, more directly to the New York tri-state region. As time progressed, and technology improved to the point where the frequency and intensity of enemy attacks became greater, the need for fortifications near and on Long Island became of fundamental military importance. With the outbreak of war against the British, forts were constructed on Long Island at Lloyd Neck, Fort Salonga, Huntington, Setauket, Smith Point (Shirley), Southampton, and Sag Harbor.

During the War of 1812 a fort existed near Port Jefferson Harbor known as Fort Nonsense, since it only brandished one 32-pound gun, which did not prevent a British raid.

During the Spanish-American War in 1898, Fort Terry on Plum Island, Fort Michie on Gull Island,

and Fort H. G. Wright on Fisher's Island were in operation to protect the waterways approaching New York and coastal Connecticut and Rhode Island.

With the development of airpower in the years before World War I, many camps and air bases were added across Long Island. The air bases at Hazelhurst (later Roosevelt) and Mitchel Field grew up in the vicinity of Garden City and Mineola. Lufberry Field was an army air service training facility at Massapequa. Camp Mills at Mineola and Camp Upton at Yaphank were training centers for military personnel.

World War II brought increasing threats of airpower and submarine attacks to the shores of the United States. Roosevelt and Mitchel Fields were again pressed into service, as was Camp Upton for new recruits. Out at Montauk, Camp Hero was built in 1942. This facility, along with Forts Terry, H. G. Wright, Michie and others, made up what was known as the Eastern Coastal Defense Shield, designed to protect the eastern shores of the country.

With the development of the Cold War in the years soon after World War II, Nike anti-aircraft missile sites were established at several Long Island locations—Amityville, Farmingdale, Brookhaven, Rocky Point, Hicksville, Oyster Bay, Huntington, Lloyd Harbor, Lido Beach. Named for "Nike," the mythical Greek goddess of victory, the missiles were intended to defend against attack by newly developed jet aircraft.

By the early 1970s, sophisticated technology quickly made dinosaurs out of the Nike missiles as well as the need for BOMARC (Boeing and Michigan Aerospace Research Center) at the former Suffolk County Air Base at Westhampton. With the development of satellite technology, the need for coastal defense installations such as Camp Hero became obsolete.

*An American Gibraltar* is an examination of the hamlet of Montauk, Long Island as it rose from a tranquil and desolate outpost for farm animals to a formidable Rock of Gibraltar, fortified by armed forces to help protect not only Long Islanders but neighboring coastal ports and cities such as New London, New Haven, and New York City. Montauk's role in each conflict, from the Indian wars of the 1600s to the Cold War years following World War II, varied in intensity, but its overall contribution to the fabric of American history serves to enhance the fact that Montauk has been and continues to be a very special place with a truly remarkable history.

CHAPTER **1**

# The Montaukett Indians

THE MONTAUKETTS WERE Algonquian-speaking Native Americans who lived on eastern Long Island. They were people of the sea who constructed boats and canoes of all sizes. As early as 1653, John Winthrop noted that they "have many canoes, so great as one will carry eighty men."[1]

The Montauketts were the most powerful of all the Indian tribes on Long Island. Their enemies were the Pequots, Mohegans, and Narragansetts, all of whom inhabited lands in what later became Connecticut and Rhode Island. All of these tribes were Delawares of the Algonquian branch.

According to William Wallace Tooker (1848-1917), an authority on Long Island Indian nomenclature, it seemed that the name "Montauk" appeared in as many different spellings as the name was mentioned in various writings. For example: Meantaucutt, 1656; Meantaquit, 1660; Meantauket, 1666; Meantucket, 1668; Menataukett, 1672; Meantaukut, 1674; Meuntaukut, 1676; Mantack, 1692.[2] The name is thought to mean, "Unto the fort-place/high land."

Closely related to the Montauketts on Long Island were the Shinnecocks, the Manhassets, and the Corchaugs. The Shinnecocks inhabited the land just west of the Montauketts, which is the present Shinnecock Hills region. The Manhassets lived on Shelter Island, and the Corchaugs were on Long Island's North Fork. If danger threatened any one of these groups, the others would band together to defend their lands.

With the arrival of white settlers from East Hampton in 1648, the Montauketts taught them how to hunt, trap, fish, and how to harvest whales. Settlers looking to venture out to sea sought the Montauketts for their skills as whalers.

Before the arrival of white settlers, an Indian fort existed at the extreme western end of Montauk and overlooked Napeague Harbor at a place known as Nominicks. This structure could be considered the first type of military defense on the Montauk Peninsula. In 1661 a new fort was known to exist on what is now Fort Hill, situated just below the present Montauk Manor.

The Montauketts were unlike the Indians of other regions, such as the Southwest, Midwest, and Northwest. They made no pottery, blankets, or beadwork. They are best remembered for their manufacture of wampum. Made from clam or periwinkle shells, it was used as a form of money in dealings between the Indians and the settlers.

There was some concern for the safety of the settlers when they arrived on Montauk, but there was no reason for them to fear. According to former East Hampton historian Jeannette Edwards Rattray, "[N]ot a drop of blood was ever shed in anger between the Montauk Indians and their new white neighbors."[3]

The Pequots ceased to be a threat to the tribes of Long Island when on March 25, 1637 a group of eighty Mohegans and eighty men from Hartford attacked the Pequots at Mystic, Connecticut, virtually wiping out the village in a bloody massacre. After the battle, a Montaukett named Wyandanch (1571-1659), acting on behalf of his brother, Long Island's great sachem ("chief") Poggatacut, and on behalf of the sachems of the neighboring tribes, went to Saybrook, Connecticut to meet with English settler Lion Gardiner (1599-1663) to propose an alliance between the English and the Montauketts against the Narragansetts and other tribes that might threaten the Montauketts. Gardiner agreed. Montaukett sachem Wyandanch showed his appreciation by enabling Gardiner to purchase, on May 3, 1639, what is now Gardiner's Island, an island of about 3,500 acres between the east end towns of East Hampton and Southold.

The massacre of the Pequots enabled Niantic sachem Ninigret to gain power. He and the Niantics (a branch of the Narragansetts, also called Nehantics), along with the Narragansetts, began to formulate an attack against the English settlers and proposed their plans to the Montauks and Shinnecocks. However, Wyandanch informed his friend Lion Gardiner about the plan and it failed. This only served to enrage Ninigret more against the Montauks.

Early in 1638 Ninigret and eighty followers came to see Wyandanch to convince him to ally himself with the Niantics. Ninigret hoped to sever a newly-formed alliance between the Montauketts and the English before it had the chance to strengthen. Wyandanch refused. In response the Niantics raided several neighboring villages, which convinced some of the older Montauketts to accept Ninigret's terms.

Warriors from Block Island who were allies of the Narragansetts engaged in a battle with the Montauketts. They met each other midway between Block Island and Montauk Point:

> [T]he Block Indians first saw the others at a distance to the Westward in the Glade of the Moon while the light of the moon which was in the same direction prevented their being seen by the Montauk Indians. The former faced about, returned and drew up their canoes on the Island; the Montauk Indians landed and fell into the ambush that was laid for them…The Montauk Indians were nearly all killed; a few were protected by the English and brought away.[4]

In August 1653, Ninigret and his Niantics led a surprise attack on Montauk, killing some thirty Montauketts at a site known as Massacre Valley, located at the foot of present Montauk Manor. This proved to be the bloodiest battle on the lands of Montauk. The war lasted several years with the loss of many Montauketts. Montauk itself was invaded and the Nehantics "would have extirpated the whole tribe, if they had not found protection in the humanity of the people of East Hampton. The Montauketts were obliged to abandon their villages and to flee for refuge to East Hampton where they were kindly received, sustained, and protected. They continued to reside in that town for several years, before they deemed it safe to return to Montauk."[5]

Thomas James, minister of the East Hampton Presbyterian Church, called for assistance. In 1655 the Commissioners sent military supplies to East Hampton and the Montauketts. An armed ship stood ready in Block Island Sound, commanded by Captain John Youngs. He had orders to attack and destroy Ninigret's forces should they attempt an attack on Montauk. War appeared to subside by 1657, but disagreements continued.

In 1651, sachem Poggatacut died and his brother Wyandanch became grand sachem of Long Island. The proprietors of East Hampton, concerned that their future purchase of Montauk would be jeopardized if Ninigret controlled the Montauketts, sent supplies to Wyandanch on August 23, 1654 to help protect

Ninigret, Chief of the Niantics, crossed the Long Island Sound from Connecticut and led an attack on the Montauketts in 1653, killing about thirty of them near the site of the present Montauk Manor. The war lasted for several years. This portrait is dated to 1681, artist unknown.

the Montauketts. A year later, Wyandanch was accused by Ninigret of murdering a group of Englishmen near the shores of Long Island, of assaulting Ninigret on Block Island and killing several of his men, plus other charges. Wyandanch was acquitted of any wrongdoing.

In view of the defeat of Wyandanch in bloody wars between eastern and northern Indians against the English, Lion Gardiner tried to alert the New England colonies to the danger of allowing Ninigret to continue to antagonize the Montauketts,. Gardiner's pleas fell on deaf ears, since the Commissioners at Boston chose not to get involved.

Having learned that Ninigret was at Block Island, Wyandanch went there with a great number of Montauketts and killed about thirty Indians. In retaliation, Ninigret went to Montauk and destroyed much Indian property, killed many warriors, and captured fourteen women, one of whom was Wyandanch's daughter Quashawam. Among the dead was her bridegroom. Supposedly, Quashawam's wedding had just taken place and, being in a festive mood, the Montauketts were not vigilant when Ninigret attacked. The scene of most of the fighting, Massacre Valley, is located near present Montauk Manor behind Fort Hill. This battle was the last time blood was shed on Montauk. The ransom for Quashawam was largely raised by Lion Gardiner. To show his appreciation, in 1659 Wyandanch presented Gardiner with a deed for lands now known as the Town of Smithtown.

The Commissioners sent supplies to East Hampton, Southampton, and the Montauketts and arranged for an armed vessel to protect against any attack by Ninigret. Support for this operation was eventually discontinued and Wyandanch found himself fighting against forces vastly superior to his own. War continued between the Narragansetts and the Montauketts, but since it was confined to them alone, very little is known of actual events.

During 1658 and 1659 the spread of disease wiped out two thirds of all Indians on Long Island. In 1659 Wyandanch himself died, supposedly poisoned, but no proof of this exists in colonial records. Without their leader, the Montauketts turned to the people of East Hampton and were "hospitably

Montaukett Sachem Wyandanch, rendered by Shinnecock artist David Bunn Martine, is based on extensive research.

received, and kindly relieved and protected."[6] Surviving Indians moved to the east end of Town Pond between the homes of Lion Gardiner and Thomas James in East Hampton.

According to Seon Manley, with the death of Wyandanch, "the English lost a warm and devoted friend. His attachment for the whites...never wavering, and the commanding influence which he possessed over the Indian tribes of the island, was ever exercised to prevent any hostile movements against them."[7]

Wyandanch was a man of influence. When an Englishwoman was murdered by Indians in Southampton in 1649, all eyes fell on the Shinnecocks. Mandush, the Shinnecock sachem, refused to cooperate with the investigation, but to avoid further tension, Lion Gardiner sent Wyandanch. Through his influence and friendship with the Shinnecocks, the men responsible were captured, tried, and executed.

Wyandanch became well known across Long Island and he found himself involved in numerous land transactions. Like the name "Montauk" that was spelled in various ways, William Wallace Tooker noted examples of numerous spellings of the great sachem's name: Weandance 1642; Wiantanse or Wiantance 1644; Weyrinteynich 1645; Wyandanch 1648; Waindance 1657; Wyandance 1657; Wyandack 1659. It seems fitting that Tooker described the name as meaning, "the wise speaker or talker, from whom we could learn something."[8] The community of Wyandanch in Suffolk County, Long Island bears homage to this sage and politically deft sachem.

Richard F. (Dick) White, who was born on Montauk in 1941 and has a profound interest in the history of the Montauk community, summed up Wyandanch's significance in an interview with the author in March 2010:

> Montauk was very important in those days because it was considered the "mint". The wampum they made was of very high quality, and that was early Montauk's claim to fame. That was why Wyandanch, the Montauk sachem, had such a big say in dealing with Lion Gardiner and giving him land.[9]

After the death of Wyandanch, Ninigret and the Narragansetts grew bold in their attacks on Long Island Indians. Finally on August 6, 1660,, to protect themselves and their possessions, Wyandanch's widow, Wichikittawbut, and son, Weoncombone, with the consent of Lion Gardiner and his son David, who had been appointed by Wyandanch as guardian of his son, conveyed all of Montauk to Thomas Baker, Robert Bond, Thomas James, and thirty others of East Hampton.

When Wyancombone died in 1662, "the title of Sachem disappeared and the rule of the Indians was over even as a line upon a piece of paper."[10] By 1665 New York Governor Richard Nicolls declared there was no longer a "grand sachem" of Long Island.[11]

From 1661 to 1687 various groups of men from East Hampton acquired all of Montauk from the Indians, although the Montauketts continued to live at Indian Field, located east of Lake Montauk. The

Lion Gardiner was painted fighting in the Pequot War by artist Charles Stanley Reinhart (1844-1896) ca.1890. The defeat of the Pequots was instrumental in cementing good relations between Lion Gardiner and the Montaukett Indians.

East Hampton proprietors used the land to pasture their cattle, sheep, goats and horses. According to Robert Hefner, historic preservation advisor to the Village of East Hampton, "Raising livestock, especially cattle, seems to have been the predominant aspect of East Hampton's agrarian economy. Undoubtedly the thousands of acres of pasture at Montauk was the major resource for this economy."[12]

The English came to view the Montauketts as a nuisance and a hindrance to the development of East Hampton Town. In 1665, at Hempstead, Long Island, Governor Richard Nicolls (1624-1672) proclaimed the Duke's Laws, which were primarily directed at English and Dutch settlers but also imposed restrictions on the Indians' ways of life in order to avoid conflicts that could escalate into violence over land deals, damage to crops and livestock, and the sale of alcohol. Governor Nicolls also was concerned about damage to Indian property and to the Indians themselves, so the Laws required settlers to compensate the Indians for such damages or losses.

With the English purchase of lands from Hither Hills to Fort Pond in 1662, it was agreed that East Hampton held the "exclusive right of purchase for all of the remaining Montaukett land" from Fort Pond to Montauk Point. The Indians were permitted to build wigwams and use the land at Hither Woods, plus "graze their livestock east of Fort Pond, between the harvest and the spring planting".[13]

Early Long Island historian Benjamin Thompson described the demise of the Montauketts on Montauk:

*In return for the friendly bearing of their Indian neighbors, the white people proffered them their protection at all times, particularly when threatened by their savage enemies of Narragansett and Block Island, who for many years kept the natives of Montauk in a constant state of fear and alarm. To reciprocate this protection, the settlers were allowed the pasturage of Montauk for their cattle, and the pre-emptive right, in the purchase of the remaining lands, was secured to them. The original agreement was entered into May 22, 1658, and in the ensuing winter a fatal epidemic destroyed more than half the native inhabitants, while Wyandanch himself lost his life by poison, secretly administered. The remnant of the Montauks, both to avoid the fatal malady, and to escape the danger of invasion, in their then forlorn and weakened state, fled in a body to their white neighbors, who received and entertained them for a considerable period. Wyoncombone, having succeeded his father, and being a minor, divided the government with his widowed mother. Lyon Gardiner and his son David acted as guardians to the young chief, by request of his deceased father.*

On Aug. 1, 1660, the widow, styled the squa-sachem, and her infant son, confirmed the lands on Montauk to the original purchasers, described as extending from sea to sea, and the easternmost parts thereof to the bounds of Easthampton, for the consideration of £100, payable in ten equal annual installments, in Indian corn, or good wampum, at six to a penny.[14]

By 1665 the Montauketts were involved with the English in tending cattle on Montauk, but many had relocated to East Hampton where they found work as laborers or servants.

The battles and other events of the French and Indian War never reached the shores of Montauk, or Long Island for that matter, but on July 5, 1757 the East Hampton Town Trustees agreed to send four pounds of powder and eight pounds of lead for bullets to Third House, to be maintained by James Loper. If necessary, Loper would supply the Montauketts with the ammunition in the event of an enemy attack. Though these precautions were taken, no attack occurred.

# CHAPTER 2

# The American Revolution

FOLLOWING THE BOSTON Tea Party on December 16, 1773, which was in response to the Tea Act of 1773, which the colonists believed violated their right to be taxed only by their own elected representatives, the British responded by closing the harbor until the destroyed tea had been paid for. This only set off more protests and eventually ignited the American Revolution in 1775.

Eastern Long Islanders, aware of the conflict, became concerned for their own safety and the possible plunder of the herds of cattle and sheep kept on Montauk. On June 8, 1775 Thomas Wickham asked the Provincial Congress if they would pay for any animals removed by the British in the event an attack could not be prevented.[15]

Everett Rattray, longtime editor of the *East Hampton Star*, noted that, thanks to the early settlers on the East End, the terrain of the Town of East Hampton was mostly bare, with almost all trees removed. By the time of the Revolution, "cattle were driven into the glacial kettle holes to hide them from the eyes of the lookouts at the mastheads of the beef-hungry Royal Navy; the Island was close to being the vast treeless rolling plain that the Montauk communal pasture was, well within living memory."[16]

On July 5, 1775, the Town of East Hampton advised the New York Provincial Congress that about 2,000 cattle and as many as 4,000 sheep lay unprotected on the fields of Montauk. The town requested that troops be sent to protect them. On July 27, 1775 General George Washington (1732-1799) notified East Hampton authorities that a British fleet from Boston was headed to Long Island with three men of war, nine transports, and six hundred men, and that precautions should be taken to preserve the cattle on Montauk. On August 9th it was agreed by the Trustees of East Hampton "not to have any Cattle go on to Meantauk till ordered as they were brought off on account of a fleet that appeared off ye point and went to fishers Island after Cattle."[17] So the cattle were protected but not the sheep. This British fleet also plundered Gardiner's Island on August 11th.

In August 1775 Congress recommended the removal of livestock from Gardiner's Island and Plum Island. Later that month, it was proposed to the Provincial Congress to keep an eye on Queens County as well since there were indications that the British might look to remove livestock from there as well.

On September 25, 1775 the Committee of Safety notified East Hampton and Southampton of a potential attack from another fleet of British ships from Boston.[18] However, the attack never came and calm prevailed on the East End for the remainder of the year.

On March 6, 1776 guards were stationed on Montauk to protect the cattle and sheep. In July 1776, Colonel Henry B. Livingston (1716-1778), a signer of the Declaration of Independence, was put in command by order of General Washington. Livingston "used every exertion to preserve the stock from falling into the enemy's hands."[19]

This earliest portrait of George Washington, painted in 1772 by Charles Wilson Peale (1741-1827), shows him in uniform as colonel of the Virginia Regiment. Washington was aware of the threat to eastern Long Island's cattle at Montauk during the Revolution and did what he could until the Battle of Long Island caused him to transfer men to the fighting in Brooklyn.

Following the British evacuation of Boston on March 17, 1776, word was sent to East Hampton by the Provincial Congress of a possible attack on Long Island. With a very short supply of men and munitions on Montauk, Congress sent 1,000 pounds of powder and 4,000 pounds of lead to Huntington for the use of Suffolk County.[20] This did not satisfy the East End and requests continued for troops and supplies to protect the Montauk Peninsula.

Captain John Hulbert of Bridgehampton and Sag Harbor was a captain of militia and in July 1775 was assembling a militia for General Philip Schuyler's army. The people of East Hampton supplied them with arms, ammunition and provisions and requested these forces be sent to Montauk. Captain Hulbert and his small army of sixty-nine men headed to Montauk, but upon seeing the size of the enemy fleet off Montauk Point decided that their own numbers were insufficient. Help was requested from East Hampton.

One volunteer was Captain John Dayton (1727-1825) of the First Regiment of Minutemen in Suffolk County, along with forty other local farmers. When Dayton and his men reached the Shepherd's Neck area of Montauk later in July, the British ships had moved into Fort Pond Bay.

Dayton had a plan, which was described by Henry P. Hedges (1817-1911) in 1849 on the occasion of the Town of East Hampton's 100th anniversary:

> The Captain thought he could prevent their landing and save the cattle. He offered to lead forty of his neighbors, if so many would go, and save their flocks. Forty volunteered to accompany the Captain, and they marched on to Montauk. He selected a hill, marched over it at the head of his company- descended into a hollow, where he was out of sight from the fleet. Shifting the position of his men, and each exchanging his coat, he again led them back, through a hollow, unobserved by the fleet, to the starting place and over the hill; and thus the company continued their march over and around the hill. The manouvre [sic] was calculated to produce this impression upon the fleet that a large army were marching and encamping in the vale below. Whether this stratagem was the cause or not, the result was that the British did not land and the flocks were saved."[21]

The British, thinking there was a large army defending Montauk, elected not to attempt a landing and instead raided nearby Gardiner's Island. This proved to be no contest as there were only three people on the island at the time—an overseer, a slave, and an Indian woman. The island's proprietor at the time was four-year old John Lyon Gardiner (1770-1816), the previous one, David Gardiner having died in 1774.

It is believed that Dayton's clever plan gave rise to the phrase "turncoat."

The John Hulbert flag, said to have been made in 1775, was found in a house once owned by Captain John Hulbert. No proof exists that it was made by him and any dates connected to it have been contested as a result of recent scientific studies of the cloth.

Captain Dayton's house was located two miles west of the present village of East Hampton, at the head of Dayton's Creek, a tributary of Georgica Pond, and was—

*an inviting location for the miscreant and coward to attack or plunder...It was once attacked in the night by the enemy, and while he was in the act of lighting a candle, a musket was discharged at him...the ball missed him and passed in the beam of his weaver's loom. Putting his little son [Josiah] out of the back door, in the midst of a deep snow, and directing him to flee for shelter and safety, he...returned the enemy's fire, and withdrew in the house. He immediately began to call all imaginary names, as if he had a regiment of assistance...The shot, or the deception, or perhaps both, were successful. The enemy retired and left the marks of blood behind them.*[22]

Capturing New York was primary to British plans, for this would effectively separate the colonies of New England from those in the south and would give the British control of shipping on the Hudson River.

The towns of eastern Long Island pleaded for help from the Provincial Congress against British attacks, but no aid came, so Long Islanders did what they could to defend themselves.

On April 7, 1776 enemy ships were seen in Gardiner's Bay and on the ocean. A company was formed with Captain John Dayton in charge. The following is a letter sent from a member of his company, Ichabod Raynor of West Hampton, to his mother from Montauk on August 9, 1776:

*After my duty to you, this may serve to let you know that I am in good health at present and hope these lines will find you all in the injoyment of the same blessing. I should be glad if you would send me cloth enough for a pair of trowsers, by George Howell, and I will get Wm. Brewster to make them. I like being a soldier very well. It is a healthy time in the camp. I shall expect to see you in about a month.*[23]

During the spring of 1776 a battle took place off Montauk Point between American forces under Commodore Esek Hopkins (1718-1802) and British forces who were attempting to steal the horses and cattle from Montauk. Though no details of the confrontation exist, John Lion Gardiner wrote in 1798 that his family on Gardiner's Island was scared and moved to East Hampton for safety.[24] The bluffs at Montauk were reportedly used for firing practice with cannons by both American and British warships.

There was increasing concern to protect an estimated 100,000 cattle and a larger number of sheep on Long Island, so on July 20, 1776, twenty-five percent of the Long Island militia was assigned to round them up for purchase by the Continental Army. [25]

Any attention to protection of cattle quickly came to a close when it was reported that British General Lord William Howe (1729-1814), after evacuating Boston, planned to use New York as a new base of operations. The Battle of Long Island took place at Brooklyn on August 27, 1776. It was the first major battle of the Revolution following the Declaration of Independence. American forces were outnumbered four to one and soon beat a hasty retreat. General Howe and his experienced soldiers easily overpowered the scattered and inexperienced Americans. Under cover of darkness on August 29th General George Washington and his forces safely retreated across the East River to Manhattan, effectively ending the battle.

The threat to the cattle on Montauk was noted by Colonel Livingston in a letter to General Washington on August 30th:

> On Thursday Last I received an Express from Captain Davis stationed at Mountauk Point notifying me, that he had discovered three sails of the Enemy making for the Point, that they had hoisted out their Boats to the Number of ten or twelve he supposed with design to land and Carry off stocks. After giving the orders I thought necessary to Captain Roe and Griffin, I set out for the Point. On my arrival in the Evening at Captain Davis'es station I found three Vessels which I took to be Frigates from twenty to thirty guns, a Brig we immagined a Prize, and a small Sloop. Close in with the Land; at 7 Oclock in the Evening one of the Frigates the Brig and the Sloop made for the Continent south west of New London where they anchored under the shore; the other two ships Bore away for Block Island.[26]

With the loss at Brooklyn, all of Long Island soon fell under British control. Governor William Tryon (1729-1788) ordered troops to occupy all of the towns on Long Island. A couple of weeks later at Sag Harbor, huge crowds assembled at the docks awaiting passage to Connecticut in order to escape British occupation. According to writer Averill Geus, "It is estimated that 171 heads of East Hampton families sought refuge in Connecticut during the war."[27]

Southampton, East Hampton, Sag Harbor and other towns were soon occupied by British forces that, in most cases, dealt unkindly with the townsfolk and resources of Long Island. To complicate matters, whaleboat warfare was conducted from Connecticut. Under cover of darkness men would row across Long Island Sound to Long Island to ransack homes and attack people. Wrote Geus, "It was a war of retribution and plunder and often a fight between the big landowners and the small farmers and had nothing to do with the Revolutionary War at all."[28] Chaos often prevailed on Long Island's east end, including Montauk.

An entry appeared in the Journal of the East Hampton Trustees in October 1777 telling of the British fleet in the bay and a ship stationed in an area thought to be Fort Pond Bay. The cattle taken then by the British were paid for, however the Trustees wrote to the Captain of the vessel in October, complaining of them taking the stock at such a low price.[29]

Although Congress was certainly angry over the loss of the cattle and wrote to the authorities of East Hampton and Southold to request that any remaining cattle from Gardiner's and Plum Islands be removed, the government was reluctant to provide troops on the east end of Long Island since they were needed in critical locations elsewhere.

One whaleboat attack on May 23, 1777 did prove positive for the American cause. In response to

British attacks on numerous Connecticut towns, Lt. Col. Return Jonathan Meigs (1740-1823) gathered a group of 170 men and departed Guilford, Connecticut for Long Island. Landing first at Southold on Long Island's North Fork, they carried their boats across land to Peconic Bay and sailed for Sag Harbor, which Colonel Meigs knew contained British supplies in great numbers. The troops came ashore about four miles from town and made their approach on foot. Meigs' forces destroyed the supplies and killed or captured British soldiers, all without the loss of a single man! Sag Harbor saw much destruction of homes, businesses, wharves and ships during the course of the British occupation.

Though Montauk and the rest of Long Island were under British control for the remainder of the Revolution, East Hampton still found the courage to protest and involve itself in underground activity. On August 23, 1779, the town trustees "agreed to send one man to New York to inform General Tryon that the Kings Troops hath taken a number of cattle off the land of Montauk by way of plunder and sent one man to Montauk to watch the Motion of the King's Ships."[30] Also, as late as June 18, 1781 town trustees "agreed to send one man to Montauk, and for him to stay there several days in order to guard our stock."[31]

A British fleet anchored in Gardiner's Bay in September 1780 and remained there until the following March. Notable among the fleet were the *Royal Oak,* with 74 guns and commanded by Vice Admiral Mariot Arbuthnot (1711-1794); the *London,* 90 guns, Rear Admiral Samuel Graves (1713-1787); the *Culloden,* 74 guns, under a Captain Sweeny; the *Bedford,* 74 guns, Captain Edmund Affleck (1725-1788); and the *Prudent,* 74 guns, under Sir Charles Ogle.

A significant British setback was the loss of the 74-gun ship *Culloden,* commanded by Captain Nisbet Balfour (1744-1823), off Montauk on January 23, 1781. The ship was 170 feet long, 47 feet wide, and had three decks with a crew of about 650. When three French ships were seen off Newport, Rhode Island moving toward Long Island, presumably to aid the American cause, the order was given for the *Culloden* and two other ships—the *Bedford* and the *America*—to chase them off. However, a blinding snowstorm moved in and the ships made an attempt to head for the open sea. The *Bedford* and *America* made it to safety, but the *Culloden* struck at Shagwong Reef near Montauk Point, opening a hole in its hull. The ship attempted to reach calmer waters in Fort Pond Bay but ran aground off what was then known as Will's (now Culloden) Point. Attempts to refloat the vessel were fruitless. To prevent the Americans from salvaging the ship's guns, the British burned the vessel to the waterline, taking what they could with them. There were no casualties. The site of the wreck was placed on the National Register of Historic Places in 1979.

An interesting tale is related by Everett Rattray regarding the Reverend Dr. Samuel Buell of East Hampton's Presbyterian Church. While Admiral Arbuthnot and his fleet were anchored in Gardiner's Bay, keeping a wary eye on a French fleet anchored near Newport, Rhode Island, he invited a number of "the gentry of East Hampton" to dine with him aboard his ship, *Royal Oak.* Reverend Buell and Colonel Abraham Gardiner were among the guests, who "dined on curries, including something known as The Devil. Dr. Buell is said to have observed archly that with such spicy food, fruit, and women aboard ship, the consequences might be untoward. Admiral Arbuthnot responded that there were no Eves aboard, a slander on East Hampton's fairest."[32]

Contending not only with the feisty Americans, the British had to deal with deserters from their own ranks, too. John Lyon Gardiner wrote, "Some time in the spring of '80 there came a party of the British, about fifteen or twenty, under Lieutenant Derby, into Amagansett, on their way to Montauk after deserters, as it was a very common thing for soldiers to get off to Connecticut that way."[33]

An incident took place one day at Third House, Montauk, where some British soldiers came

Launched in 1776, the Culloden, a 74-gun British ship of the Royal Navy, was named for the Battle of Culloden (1746) in Scotland. The ship ran aground in a heavy snowstorm at Fort Pond Bay, Montauk, on January 23, 1781. After salvaging what they could, the British burned it to the waterline. There was no loss of life. (Montauk Point Lighthouse Museum)

demanding food. The woman inside, at work in the kitchen, was determined not to give away any of the meager provisions on hand. She grabbed a dipper and, filling it with very hot water from a kettle, tossed it in the direction of the intruders shouting, "Come in if you dare!" The soldiers departed, empty handed and hungry.[34]

Several Montaukett Indians served in the Revolution, some with John Paul Jones on the U. S. S. *Ranger*, and Sam Beaman with Captain Joseph Conkling aboard the privateer *Revenge* in 1777-78.[35]

In December 1781, the East Hampton Trustees assigned what portion of forty tons of hay requisitioned by the British would be supplied by each man in the town. The Montauketts complained to the British that the proprietors on Montauk had impounded their cattle. The possibility of an uprising grew. Two Trustees went to British headquarters at Jamaica, New York to respond to the charges. As a result, a letter was sent by the Indian Affairs Superintendent to the Town Trustees which stated:

*I am therefore authorized to require you to take these matters into consideration and that you will afford these poor people such liberty and indulgence as they have reasonably required as it is his Majestie's pleasure to give all protection and countenance to those who by their fidelity are entitled to the favor of the government.*[36]

# CHAPTER 3

# The War of 1812

FOR YEARS AFTER the American Revolution the British harassed American shipping and by 1812 had impressed about 2,500 American soldiers into the British navy. In response the United States declared war on June 19, 1812. On Long Island plans were immediately made for the defense of Sag Harbor. British ships were once again anchored in Gardiner's Bay by June 2, 1813 but no attempts were made to land. Among the British ships off the coast were the *Ramillies, Orpheus, Maidstone, Sylph, Thunderer, Plantagenet* and the *Boxer.* Led by Commodore Sir Thomas Hardy (1769-1839), a small group of British sailors made raids at night with little impact.

With the British fleet blockading Gardiner's Bay, Henry Packer Dering, federal agent at the Port of Sag Harbor, wrote to Brigadier General Abraham Rose (1765-1843) of Bridgehampton that "the enemy landed...at Gardiner's Island and took off a number of head of cattle, and that a number of ships now remain laying off Gardiner's Point."[37]

A week later, on June 12th, General Rose, who was commander in charge of the defense of Sag Harbor during the war, responded to "Mr. Deering":

> *We are at present in a very disagreeable situation, the enemy very plenty in our waters (eight ships in number yesterday) have taken cattle and sheep from Gardiner's Island, have been on Montauk twice for wood and water, and have taken ten cattle. No alarm has yet been made, owing partly for want of information in time and partly perhaps from the opposition the people of Easthampton have to making any resistence, being as they say impossible for us to defend the place without a standing force...*
>
> *considering that, our militia, even the most easterly regiment, is scattered from twelve to fifty miles from Montauk, it will be seen that, in one quarter of the time necessary to get the militia there, that the enemy can easily effect their purpose and be off...*
>
> *Should we remain as we now are there is no doubt that the enemies ships will make Montauk a place of rendezvous for supplies the whole season...*
>
> *Many are of opinion that the cattle ought to be removed from Montauk, but the owners generally say they cannot keep them otherways. Some individuals who had but few have taken them off; there are probably nearly two thousand yet there.*

*It seems the British left pay for what they took which I consider a bad thing, as it has a tendency to cool our patriotism.*[38]

On the night of July 10, 1813 several boats left the fleet and sailed for Sag Harbor. Having been spotted in time, cannon fire from Turkey Hill in Sag Harbor drove the invaders away. On July 28, 1813, a contingent of British forces came ashore at Little Gull Island where a lighthouse had been built only six years before. They approached keeper Giles Holt and demanded he extinguish the light. When Giles refused, the British removed the lamps from the lantern. Being only about fourteen miles northwest of Montauk Point, the British presence posed a threat to the cattle and sheep on Montauk.

This time Uriah Miller (1784-1859) of Second House, Montauk played a prominent and bold role. At the time, he was in charge of approximately twelve hundred cattle pastured on Montauk. After the British came ashore and carried off some of the cattle, an enraged Miller was determined to extract payment for the loss. He ordered a Montaukett Indian to take him in a canoe out to the ship of Commodore Thomas Hardy. Arriving on board and armed with a cowhide whip he was approached by an officer who demanded to know the purpose of this surprise visit. Miller said he wanted payment for his lost cattle "or he would take it out of somebody, if he had to thrash the whole English fleet."[39]

Miller was brought before the Commodore, who was both amazed and amused by Miller's audacity. Nevertheless, the Commodore paid him a fair price and declared him to be the bravest man in America. Uriah Miller continued living at Second House keeping a watchful eye on the cattle and sheep until 1826. He died in 1859, aged 74.

With the British fleet anchored nearby, there was also concern that they might attempt to take over the Montauk Point Lighthouse. On April 3, 1813, Joseph H. Hand of East Hampton, who had been a minuteman in the American Revolution and served at the Battle of Long Island in 1776 with the 4th New York Regiment, wrote to Nathaniel Huntting expressing his concern (punctuation added by the author):

*Thinking you may have heard various rumours respecting these ships that have been off Montauk 3 or 4 days past, and believing you would be grateful to hear something that may be depended upon, I have taken the liberty to address a few lines to you to that effect.*

*On the morning of the 31st of March a large Brig captured 2 sloops and immediately stood to sea. The following evening came in and anchored off the Point a 74 gunship under French Coulers but undoubtedly a British ship. On the morning of the 1st April was calm and her barges busily employed in sounding and viewing Shagwananock reef. One of the barges went and viewed the boiling spring but did not venture any further. About 1 o'clock p.m. a frigate came in from sea, made several signals for the 74 when she immediately got under weigh and they both stood off. April 2nd came in 2 Frigates and captured a schooner outward bound. They then proceeded to Block island where they now are. [T]here is now 2 Frigates bearing South from the light. They are standing in for the land- we shall probably be visited from them soon. I could write you much more respecting them but not having time at present I cannot detail any more except they do not molest the fishermen."*[40]

Mysteriously, after Hand filed this report he was never heard from again.

During the War of 1812, Vice-Admiral Sir Thomas Hardy led the fleet that escorted and transported the British army that captured several portions of the east coast of Maine. He is best known locally for his meeting with the spirited Uriah Miller of Montauk. The painting is by Robert Evans.

During the war the lighthouse was used as a central landmark for the British fleet which was attempting to set up a blockade of the Long Island Sound. By March 1813 the blockade extended from Montauk Point to the Deep South in the Mississippi River Delta.

Fearing for the safety of the lighthouse and keeper Jared Hand and family, on January 3, 1814, Henry Packer Dering wrote to the Secretary of the Treasury, Albert Gallatin, requesting "spy glasses" for the keepers at Montauk Point and Little Gull Island Lighthouses to observe the movements of British ships.[41]

Concern for a takeover of the lighthouse and the removal of its equipment by British forces, Dering wrote again to the Secretary of the Treasury, Alexander Dallas on March 2, 1815: "I saved all the oil and apparatus from the destruction of the enemy by removing them, which will be carried back and reinstalled as soon as the roads are passable."[42] At this point, Henry Baker was the keeper of the Montauk Point Lighthouse, having assumed the position on February 24, 1814. Although these precautions were taken, there is no documented evidence indicating that the lighthouse was taken over by British forces during the war.

In addition to paying for livestock at Montauk, the British also paid for cattle taken at Oyster Ponds (now Orient, Long Island). This sort of activity gives the impression that the British were basically making themselves feel at home on Long Island's East End. On August 10, 1814 the following article appeared in the *Columbian*, a New York City publication, voicing more concern for the safety of the livestock on Montauk:

*"Reinforcements have arrived in the mouth of Long Island Sound. Our informant counted on Sunday (7th) in Gardiner's Bay three ninety-gun ships, four seventy-fours, four frigates, and one brig…There was no transports or troops on board the shipping, the crews of which were sickly and were to be landed on Montauk Point to recover and recruit. Whether the ships were direct from Europe, or gathered from other parts of our coast, was not known. Montauk is common pasture for about 1,500 cattle, 1,400 sheep and 200 horses, belonging to the citizens of East Hampton, and would furnish refreshment for the well as well as for the sick, if not removed by the owner."[43]*

Around that time a letter from Sag Harbor said of the enemy: "They are permitted to come on shore and get whatever they choose within ten or twelve miles of us. The officers and crews of their war vessels are daily feasting on the rich produce of the American soil at a liberal price."[44]

During one of the British sailors' excursions ashore for provisions (which were purchased at market prices), Americans captured some of the crew. In response, the British attempted to arrest John Lyon Gardiner, Lord of the Manor at Gardiner's Island. Gardiner, who was a delicate, but shrewd, man, adopted the "green room defense" where he stayed in a bed with green curtains surrounded by medicine to make him look sickly. The British, not wanting to take a sick man aboard their vessel, left him.

As had occurred during the Revolutionary War, there were British deserters during the War of 1812, too. Some came from the ships *Superb* and *Endymion* which landed at Montauk. They remained on Long Island.[45] This is described in a letter from Doctor Ebenezer Sage of Sag Harbor in 1814:

> *Yesterday two deserters from here [Sag Harbor[ from the Superb. They took a boat from one of the ship's tenders and landed about twenty miles from this [Montauk] and traveled nearly all the distance without entering a house, having been told that the American government would send all deserters back to be hung...The people furnished these poor tars with some money, and they have started for New York.*[46]

It seems these deserters gave Long Islanders a terrible fright by declaring that sixteen ships with a large army would come through Long Island Sound and attack New York City. However, this never happened.[47]

An interesting story surrounds one of the deserters, Thomas H. Deverell, the son of an English duke. He was a well educated gentleman who held the rank of lieutenant aboard the British ship *Endymion*. While at sea and involved in a card game with the ship's commander, an argument ensued during which he struck the commander in the face. Fearing serious punishment, perhaps even death, he came ashore on Montauk. Subsequently, during the years 1816-1818 he taught school at Babylon, married, and took up residence in Patchogue, passing away about 1860.[48]

In general, Long Island did not suffer the hardships brought on by the British during the American Revolution, and the cattle on Montauk "appears to have suffered but little by depredations of the British fleet in 1812-15. At least there is no note thereof."[49]

# CHAPTER 4

# The Civil War

THOMAS EDWARDS IN his "Reminiscences of Old East Hampton" recalled a wartime scene at Montauk:

> *"I remember when Fort Sumter was fired upon. About that time a man came here selling maps, who was suspected of being a Southerner and a spy. It was said that he had been down to Fort Pond Bay, Montauk, looking up a landing place for the rebels, so they might march straight through to New York. We children imagined how they would look marching through Pantigo [in East Hampton] as we saw so many pictures of soldiers in uniform in the schoolroom and elsewhere in those days."*[50]

The Montauk Point Lighthouse was renovated shortly before the war began, and within the inside wall of the tower is a plaque installed at that time listing the members of the U. S. Lighthouse Committee in 1860. In a telling reflection of how the war was to split the United States military, the plaque includes two future Union Generals, A. A. Humphreys and Joseph Totten, Confederate General Howell Cobb and Confederate Admiral Raphael Semmes, remembered as commander of the Southern raider *Alabama*.

Confederate ships looking for Union merchant ships were known to be as close as ninety miles from the Montauk Point Lighthouse.

The *Tacony*, a Confederate cruiser, captured a number of Union vessels in its brief career. Among its conquests was the *Isaac Webb*, bound from Liverpool, England for New York with about 650 passengers. It was captured on June 20, 1863 about 75-miles off the shores of Montauk and released on payment of a $40,000 bond.

There were only two enrolled residents on Montauk at the time of the Civil War and both were drafted. Both were Montaukett Indians: Stephen Talkhouse Pharoah, and William Fowler, Jr.[51] Pharoah (1819-1879) was a former whaler and forty-niner. Though an Indian, he served with the 29th U. S. Colored Troops. Pharoah lived in what was known as Indian Field on Montauk and was well known to all in East Hampton. the nickname "Talkhouse" was given to him for reasons unknown or by whom.

Jonathan Allen Miller of the Springs lost an arm during a naval battle while aboard the *Oneida*, which had been involved in naval engagements against Confederate forces near New Orleans, at Mobile, and on the Mississippi River from 1862-1864. As recalled by George "Sid" Miller (1894-1986) (no relation), he "never noticed anything was missing until the captain asked him to hand him a rope." Miller later became the head keeper at the Montauk Point Lighthouse, serving there 1865-1869 and 1872-1875.

Probably the most famous member of the Montaukett tribe, Stephen "Talkhouse" Pharaoh (1819-1879 was known for his athletic ability, hiking almost every day to and from Montauk to several parts of the Hamptons to deliver mail and packages. Part of his route has been preserved as part of Long Island's Paumanok Path. (Montauk Point Lighthouse Museum)

Dating from about 1878, this is probably the first photograph of a Montaukett family. This is the Pharaoh family at Indian Fields, Montauk. (Montauk Point Lighthouse Museum)

# CHAPTER 5

# The Spanish American War

FOLLOWING THE SINKING of the ship *Maine* on February 15th in Havana Harbor, Cuba with the loss of 252 people, the United States declared war on Spain on April 21, 1898.

That same month, a U. S. Navy signal station was established at the Montauk Point Lighthouse, following reports that the Spanish fleet might attack the North American coast.

Undersecretary of the Navy Theodore Roosevelt (1858-1919) resigned his post and enlisted in the military, attaining the rank of lieutenant colonel. He organized a volunteer cavalry regiment, which become known as the Rough Riders. After fighting in the tropical heat and humidity of Cuba, many troops were afflicted with typhoid fever or yellow fever. Roosevelt demanded these men be sent home to receive proper care, but to a place remote enough to prevent the general population from being affected. Roosevelt knew Montauk well and considered it the perfect place for a quarantine center.

Military and naval experts long recognized the strategic importance of Montauk. Before Roosevelt and his troops arrived and established the quarantine center named Camp Wikoff, a Camp Baldwin enjoyed a brief existence at Montauk in July 1897. Occupied by Company A, 23rd Regiment, a group of fifteen men from the armory in the Crown Heights section of Brooklyn came with tents, equipment, and supplies via the Long Island Railroad on July 23rd. Special train cars were provided by railroad president William H. Baldwin, for whom the camp was subsequently named. At a point between Fort Pond and the ocean (about where the village is today) Camp Baldwin was established.

The place was described by the *Brooklyn Daily Eagle* as "an ideal spot for a camp, cool, dry and healthy," and next morning the men prepared for the day's drills by taking a "dip in the surf as an appetizer." Additional men arrived by midday and experiments were conducted with military kites, plus drills in practical field work. The camp was removed by evening on July 26th.[52]

Only months before the creation of Roosevelt's Camp Wikoff, Montauk was described as a "natural Gibraltar, on a small scale" and under consideration as a military stronghold. The *Brooklyn Daily Eagle* described why this "natural stronghold" was vital to America's defense:

> *The entrance to Fort Pond Bay from the open Atlantic is through the unobstructed waters of Block Island Sound…Ships entering the harbor by this course need no approach nearer than five miles of land until Culloden Point is passed. In a word, unless long guns are mounted at Montauk Point and on Culloden Point a fleet approaching from the sea would be free from molestation until it dropped anchor in the unprotected waters of Fort Pond Bay.*

*As the approach to this harbor lies through the open Atlantic until within ten miles of the anchorage ground it would require but a few hours after sighting Montauk light for a fleet of warships to land a force of thousands of men on the peninsula of Montauk. Once in possession of this natural stronghold an invading force would be difficult to dislodge...*

*A line of rapid fire guns mounted on the highlands overlooking this waste of sand [at Napeague] would make a land attack from the west a matter of great difficulty... a line of batteries on the Montauk highlands could keep an overwhelming force at bay...*

*[A]n invading force in possession of Montauk would occupy an important strategic position from which land operations could be conducted on Long Island, or the eastern entrance to the [Long Island] Sound...or through Plum Gut, by way of the channel south of Gardiner's Island and Gardiner's Bay; or an attack could be made upon some exposed point on the New England coast.*[53]

In June 1898 consideration was given to creating a Montauk Army Corps at the Great Plain, located between Fort Pond and Lake Montauk (then known as Lake Wyandanee), with nearby Fort Pond Bay acting as a harbor. The weather was thought to be beneficial, as was the overall environment, with surf bathing, panoramic views, and fresh, pure air. At that time a fort was already under construction at Gardiner's Point, which when combined with fortifications at Great Gull Island and Plum Island, "will make the north passage to Gardiner's Bay impregnable. The occupation of the Montauk peninsula by a large force of troops and the construction of works protecting the harbor of Fort Pond Bay would be an important addition to our coast defenses."[54]

Montauk was remote and desolate, but it provided a healthful atmosphere to promote recovery. By the time 600 members of the Sixth Calvary came to Camp Wikoff in August 1898 there was still much to be done to properly accommodate the ailing troops. Wrote Averill Geus: "[W]ells had to be dug, roads laid out, and makeshift hospitals built. No arrangements had been made for the delivery of food, and typhoid patients were placed on the damp ground to sleep without tents or blankets".[55]

To assist with the poor conditions at Camp Wikoff, women from East Hampton organized a relief corps, providing needed medicines and food. Numerous merchants at East Hampton opened auxiliary camp stores supplying food products and some buildings were converted into makeshift hospitals. Among the women in charge was Emily Warren Roebling, wife of Brooklyn Bridge builder John Roebling. These women worked as hard as any man to give aid to the ailing troops.

A humorous story was related years later by Peter Joyce of Montauk. As part of preparation for the many troops coming to Montauk, a railroad survey had to be completed. Five men rushed to accomplish the task and were finished by July 31st. To celebrate their accomplishment they went to the Montauk Inn for a few drinks. A few drinks turned into several and one of the men passed out. It was then that his buddies decided to play a trick on him. They carried him to the railroad barn where coffins were stored, placed him inside one of them and loosely nailed the lid shut. The men returned to the Inn and went to bed.

However, "the waiting coffins were picked up. By the time the boxes reached the city, the fifth surveyor had sobered up and realized his predicament. When he heard noises indicating his arrival at the city terminal, he yelled and pounded until one of the guards pried off the cover. A thoroughly infuriated but sober surveyor climbed out. The guard fainted."[56]

Camp Wikoff's pier and railroad station, located at Fort Pond Bay, Montauk, became a hub of activity during the months of military occupation in 1898. (Theodore Roosevelt Collection, Harvard College Library, R560.3.EL61-127)

The Long Island Railroad reached Montauk in December 1895. The Montauk depot became a hub of activity with the establishment of Camp Wikoff. The railroad brought a number of troops and thousands of visitors, and virtually all of the troops, dead or alive, left Montauk by train. The village of buildings set up for use by military personnel included a "post office, express package building, general store, information bureau, telegraph office, printing facility, electric light and powerhouse, and two restaurants, one of which was just a shanty known as Hungry Joe's".[57]

When Camp Wikoff was created, there was a passable road that connected the railroad station to Third House. However, the route beyond Third House leading out to the lighthouse was nothing more than a wagon trail.

On August 8, 1898 the first soldiers arrived at Camp Wikoff. The camp was named for Colonel Charles Augustus Wikoff (1837-1898), who had distinguished himself in several Civil War battles. He was killed during a charge in the Battle of San Juan Hill on July 1st.

On August 8th, the day that six hundred members of the Sixth U. S. Cavalry came (the first soldiers to arrive), there were plenty of signs of progress in the construction of Camp Wikoff:

> *Fully, three hundred men are at work laying tracks and making new road beds for additional side tracks…Carpenters are at work erecting a new express depot just east of the present railroad station…Fifty men worked all day sinking wells on the lowlands between Fort Pond and Fort Pond Bay. A big water tank is being built on Lookout Hill which will have a capacity of 25,000 gallons. Train loads of water and sewer pipes, oats, hay, straw, feed, lumber and supplies for the commissary department came to camp to-day…Stables are going up for the horses and tents are being raised rapidly.*[58]

The men of the Sixth and Ninth U. S. Cavalry arrived on the transport *Gate City* on August 13th. There was concern that the vessel was a "pest ship," containing men suffering from yellow fever. It was learned that "no yellow flag was fluttering from the foremast" and the ship was "well supplied with all that was necessary to give reasonable comfort to sick soldiers."[59]

Men assigned to the life saving stations from Montauk to Quogue maintained a constant vigil for the transport ships. As soon as one was sighted, telephone calls were made to Montauk and New York. The *Gate City* was first seen by the crew of the Mecox station near Bridgehampton.[60]

*Train loads of water and sewer pipes, oats, hay, straw, feed, lumber and supplies for the commissary department came to camp to-day…Stables are going up for the horses and tents are being raised rapidly.*[61]

On August 14, 1898 Lieutenant Colonel Theodore Roosevelt, Major General Joseph Wheeler (1836-1906), and the Rough Riders arrived at the camp via the transport *Miami*. A huge welcome awaited them. "In the ranks were many gallant men stricken by fever and bullets who had strength barely sufficient to carry their arms, but who kept their places in the line and plodded proudly along."[62]

When Roosevelt came ashore he was asked how he was feeling. He replied, "I am feeling disgracefully well… I feel positively ashamed of my appearance when I see how badly off some of my brave fellows are—Oh, but we have had a bully fight!"[63]

A general view of Camp Wikoff, looking west, shows the 8th, 10th & 2nd Infantry. (Theodore Roosevelt Collection, Harvard College Library, R560.3.EL61-104)

When interviewed shortly after landing, Roosevelt spoke about his men:

*Of course I am proud of my regiment. There was never such another. In fifty days it was raised, organized, equipped, armed, mounted, out into transports, carried to Cuba and put through two victorious fights. That's the record that I think will be hard to beat…The minute fighting began, they all took naturally to it. They scrapped by nature, I suppose."*[64]

General Wheeler said of Roosevelt,

*The thing that impressed me most about his is his absolute integrity. Some men have integrity about money, others about their personal conduct. Roosevelt has both, and, more than either, the official integrity that makes him the rare man he is…Whether in the camp or in the field, Roosevelt was to be depended on always. He is perfectly fearless, and his men follow him with absolute devotion.*[65]

Private J. Knox Green of Troop C became the first of the Rough Riders to die at Montauk. Though the cause was given as malaria, there were those who "whispered that it was yellow fever and told of the symptoms of the deadlier scourge".[66] Following Knox' death, the camp cemetery was established. Over 250 soldiers were buried on Montauk during the existence of Camp Wikoff.

Montauk native Frank (Shank) Dickinson, who was born in Third House in 1924 and now resides in East Hampton, noted that his grandparents, Phineas and Sarah Dickinson, had a farm called the Ditch Plains Farm where Colonel Roosevelt stayed for a time when he first arrived at Montauk.[67] The structure,

A uniformed Theodore Roosevelt strikes a noble pose on horseback at Camp Wikoff. (Theodore Roosevelt Collection, Harvard College Library, R560.3.EL61-021)

known as the Dickinson House, stands on Ditch Plains Road.

On August 18, 1898 Roosevelt received approval to be quartered at Third House. Theodore Conklin, proprietor of Third House, and Colonel Roosevelt developed a friendly relationship with each other. One day, Roosevelt's son Teddy was caught sliding down a haystack, totally destroying it. After repeatedly warning him not to do this, the younger Roosevelt kept on. Conklin grabbed the boy and proceeded to thrash him. While this was going on, up came Colonel Roosevelt, who shouted, "That's right! Give it to him, Captain Conklin!"[68]

Another incident involving the Colonel took place at Third House one night around midnight when a frightened servant girl woke Mrs. Conklin and said, "Young Captain H. is in the dining room, swearing something awful! I've brought out everything in the pantry, cold meat and cake and milk, but he says he's got to have a hot supper!" Mrs. Conklin got up and softly headed for the dining room where she found the captain "roaring hungry after an evening ride in the moonlight, probably with one of the sixty-five pretty nurses looking after the sick soldiers."

Suddenly Colonel Roosevelt appeared from a small office off the dining room and approached the table. With characteristic humility, he said: "I am very sorry, Mrs. Conklin, that you have been disturbed; what you have here is good enough for the President of the United States. Please go and get your rest." By morning, Captain H. was gone and was never again seen at Third House.[69]

Some of the transports that brought troops to Montauk were known as "death ships," with soldiers dying on board and being buried at sea. Those who successfully made it to Camp Wikoff "were in frightful condition on arrival at Montauk. Exhausted, emaciated, unable to walk with assistance, they virtually staggered off the transports onto the railroad pier at Fort Pond Bay."[70]

On August 19th three transports containing hundreds of sick and dying soldiers arrived at Montauk. The *Mobile*, carrying 1,600 men, had "not a baker's dozen of whom could claim a fair degree of health, and 300 of whom were dangerously ill."[71]

Also arriving was the *Seneca*, with 146 men aboard, seventy-three of whom were sick; and the *Comanche*, containing 488 troops, 114 of whom were suffering from illness.

It was decided to handle those aboard the *Mobile* first. Though existing accommodations at Camp Wikoff had been satisfactory, they became woefully inadequate in trying to manage this sudden barrage of sick troops. "Men turned aside their faces and wept when they saw the flower of young American manhood reduced to such a pass. No trumpet sounded, no brasses blared triumphal music. The silence that greeted these gallant boys…was funereal."[72]

> *The first man brought off the ship was unconscious. His form was so thin that the bones seemed to be sticking through the skin of his arms. His parched lips were drawn back from his teeth and his eyes were partly closed…Four of the regulars carried him to an ambulance and put him in. 'He's dead, isn't he?' asked a young man…'No, not dead,' replied an army surgeon, 'but he is in a bad way, indeed'.[73]*

One of the soldiers recalled, up close and personal, the horrific conditions faced by the men at Camp Wikoff:

> *It was impossible when we arrived at this camp, to see ten men in a company who were capable of performing any military duty. One could see guards walking in front of*

Third House, Montauk, is shown as it appeared ca.1900. Built in 1747 and rebuilt in 1806, Colonel Theodore Roosevelt made his headquarters here when the troops came to Camp Wikoff in 1898. (Montauk Library)

*headquarters with their heads fixed to the ground. They did not have the courage to lift their heads because of lack of strength and the torment of the fever that gripped them.*

*[Along the road leading to camp he saw] a soldier stretched on the ground in one place and another. It seemed that they were trying to establish another battleline because of the great number of men that had fallen to the ground because of the lack of strength and were not capable to continue on their way when the regiment arrived at the destined location—only one-third of them had been able to make that little three mile march.*[74]

Some men felt that Montauk was not suitable for them, since the air there was "too strong for men who had been deprived of their strength." The food was so bad that it "could not even satisfy dogs...Just to look at it in the can before eating it made many sick."[75]

Despite less than ideal conditions at the camp, on August 17th the *Brooklyn Daily Eagle* printed an uplifting story about the environment of Montauk:

> *Everybody says who visits Montauk Point, 'What air they get out here!' Of course they do. Montauk is a mere spit of land running out into the Atlantic deeps, and the wind has to wriggle itself out of shape to get to the end of it without crossing open sea and being cooled…The wind seems to be always blowing, and it comes with a tang of salt in it, yet strangely and deliciously blended with a wholesome country smell. Everything larger than a bush has been blown off from the earth. There is not a tree on the hills. From the great rolling waves of earth you look out over miles of sea. You have the transports in view as they come up from the southwest, you follow their smoke as they turn the point where the lighthouse lifts against the sky, and presently they come into sight again on the north side; then the tired, dusty and ragged men file off upon the pier and their battle days are over.*[76]

Support for the returning soldiers was demonstrated in many ways. When the auxiliary cruiser *Prairie*, carrying 520 soldiers, ran aground on the bar between Amagansett and Napeague Beach in a dense fog on the evening of August 25th, hundreds of townspeople showed up the next morning to offer assistance.

Initial efforts to refloat the vessel were unsuccessful. By the following morning all but those who were the sickest were brought ashore in surf boats. Once word of the grounding reached the local population, many responded to assist in the removal of the remaining men: "[M]en dashed into surf up to their waists to be the first to lift the soldiers from the boats and carry them up into the sand. It was an impressive scene and one never witnessed on this coast before." By noon, at high tide, the *Prairie* was hauled off.[77]

The crew of the Amagansett Life Saving Station sent out two surf boats. Hundreds soon arrived on the beach as word of the grounding spread. "The sight was certainly a strange one. Boatload after boatload of sick soldiers being brought ashore from a stranded war vessel to a strip of beach usually abandoned, but now crowded with people, who cheered and cheered each time a man was brought ashore."[78]

Even women from Amagansett were involved, bringing wagonloads of food and kitchen items. Before long, they were serving breakfasts to the men on the beach.

An interesting explanation for the grounding was given by the life savers from the stations at Amagansett and Napeague. They claimed that the Ponquogue Lighthouse, then located at Good Ground (now Hampton Bays), caused half of all shipping disasters off the coast of eastern Long Island. "When the weather is thick, it is constantly mistaken for the Montauk Point Light and captains proceed to round the point after leaving it from five to fifteen miles astern. The result is that they run into some of the numerous bars on this coast. The life savers…have advocated the removal of this light for years."[79]

An assessment of conditions at Camp Wikoff was made on August 28th and revealed that extensions to the hospital facilities were progressing rapidly. At this time, there were 520 patients in the detention hospital and 1,620 in the general hospital. All were comfortable and receiving care, though almost two-hundred in the general hospital did not have cots. However, they had "good heavy mattresses to lie on, and there are broad floors to protect them from the dampness, so that the absence of cots is not as serious a matter as it might seem." The report also pointed out that supplies were adequate but more nurses were needed.[80]

Men from the Amagansett Life Saving Station provided assistance to the transport ship *Prairie* that ran aground on August 25, 1898. This image of the station is from c. 1881. (Montauk Point Lighthouse Museum)

Despite denials of an outbreak of yellow fever at the camp, two men were confirmed to have died from the disease, "with all the symptoms…including black vomit." Steps were taken to isolate fifty-one men suffering from this affliction, including doubling the guards around the detention hospital. Food and supplies were kept at a safe distance.[81]

Although outside societies and organizations were created to collect money and food for the suffering troops, "death still continued its slaughter." Even those actively involved in providing aid saw no decrease in the mortality rate at Camp Wikoff, and they, too, cried out that Montauk was not a fit place for the soldiers.[82]

With each passing day it became more apparent that the existing facilities were inadequate to deal with the increasing numbers of arriving soldiers. The stories of poor conditions soon found their way into newspapers. The reports greatly concerned President William McKinley (1843-1901), who decided to come to Montauk to personally see the camp. When he arrived on September 3rd, Colonel Roosevelt greeted him at the Montauk railroad station, and after exchanging greetings they headed for the camp. Upon viewing the entire encampment from a hilltop, the President turned to General Joseph Wheeler and said, "This is beautiful. I think I never saw a handsomer camp."[83] Then the President made plans to visit soldiers in the hospital facilities. He said, "I want to go everywhere in the hospital. I want to see all of the boys who are sick and I want to hear from their own lips that they are comfortable. If there is anything that the country can do for these men who have suffered for it, they shall have it."[84]

He visited every ward in the general hospital and spoke to each patient. One man, very sick with fever, struggled to get to his feet when he heard that the President was approaching him. The President told him, "Don't get up, my man. Stay where you are!" But the soldier had risen to his feet and replied, "I'm sick, but not too sick to salute the President," and gave the salute as he stood "erect and motionless." McKinley shook his hand and said, "You are a brave fellow."

After a brief conversation, the soldier again saluted. In response, the President, "contrary to the regulations…lifted his right hand and gave an officer's salute. He seemed immensely pleased with the grit and soldierly qualities of the sick soldier."[85]

Then the President and his entourage went to Great Plain where he made a speech before 5,000 soldiers of the Fifth Army Corps.

> I am honored to meet the brave men who stand before me today. I bring you the gratitude of the nation, to whose history you have added by your valor a new and glorious page… You bore yourselves with supreme courage, and your personal bravery, never before excelled anywhere, has won the admiration of your fellow citizens and the genuine respect of all mankind, while your endurance under peculiar trial and suffering has given added meaning to American heroism…The brave officers and men who fell in battle and those who have died from exposure and sickness will live in immortal story, and their memories will be perpetuated in the hearts and the history of a generous people; and those who were dependent upon them will not be neglected by the Government for which they so freely sacrificed their lives.[86]

President McKinley lodged at Third House during his stay on Montauk. His overall impression of the camp was very positive: "What I saw of the care of the sick in the hospitals by those in charge and by the noble women engaged in that work was especially gratifying to me." The rest of the President's entourage echoed these sentiments.[87]

Although the President was favorably impressed with the camp's conditions, there were those with differing opinions regarding the President's visit. Edward S. Boughton, editor of the *East Hampton Star*, was blunt in his criticism:

> President McKinley's famous visit to the camp was a farce. While he shook hands with officers and was shown through the hospitals, men were dying out in the tents of the Regulars, without care and proper medical attention…If there is anyone who thinks the stories of the camp are overdrawn, we would say go there and do a little investigating on your own account. Do not ask questions of the officers, but go into the tents of the privates."[88]

It is very likely that Boughton's comments were true. Private Charles Johnson Post (1873-1956), who was an artist and journalist, wrote a letter that summer from Montauk, leaving no doubt as to the

President William McKinley visited Camp Wikoff in September 1898. He is pictured in a carriage with several unidentified men. (Theodore Roosevelt Collection, Harvard College Library, R560.3.EL61-106)

inadequate treatment he and others were receiving. He began by responding to the Surgeon General's statement that "milk and eggs were always plentiful" and "large supplies of milk, eggs, chickens, canned articles and other materials for special diet were always on hand:"[89]

*I was in that hospital...and maybe all of these things were on hand somewhere. Maybe they were, but if so they were pleasantly in the hands of someone else. I did not get them; I did not even see them- none of us did. But I saw many other things...*

*On that grass in the detention hospital...were sick men. Chills, fever, and delirium alternated with brief periods of lunacy...*

*Late in the afternoon a few blankets were distributed- I was not one of the lucky ones.*

*Then a hospital corps man appeared with a pail of soup, not much soup. It gave out before my turn came…*

*It was early afternoon before breakfast appeared- thin oatmeal, lumpy, and with some very much diluted condensed milk. I tore up some grass from the floor and swabbed out my mess cup, and in went the oatmeal to mix with the smelly remains of the mutton stew of the night before…*

*I got an egg, once. The man next to me had gotten one. He tried it. He had gotten the last in the pan. 'Here no,' he said, turning to me, 'you want an egg- it's yours if you can eat it.' He was right; he couldn't eat it and I couldn't either…*

*The only latrine was…fifty yards from the nearest tent, and from the farthest tent over a hundred yards. Men did their best to make it and at any hour of the day or night you passed them lying in the grass or making of the street, itself, a latrine…my street became a latrine from one end to the other…*[90]

However, conditions began to improve, and as the health of the soldiers got better they could be found along the beaches of Montauk, especially at the Ditch Plains Life Saving Station. Colonel Roosevelt himself extolled the virtues of a plunge in the pounding surf. Many chose to explore the beauty of Montauk, including visits to the Montauk Point Lighthouse where the keeper, Captain James Scott, proudly entertained the men. Scott certainly received many visitors that summer! Every day soldiers would come and "were enthusiastically welcomed by the old lighthouse keeper, who shows them all his curios and explains to them the mechanism of the big light…and tell them sea stories of the terrible coast on which so many good ships have left their ribs to bleach in the sun at low tide."

Colonel Roosevelt himself, with his entourage, visited the lighthouse on September 6th. He was accompanied by: James R. Church, 1st Lieutenant, Assistant Surgeon, Medal of Honor recipient; Charles L. Ballard, 2nd Lieutenant; David M. Goodrich, 1st Lieutenant, later headed Goodrich Rubber Co.; Hal Sayre, Jr., 2nd Lieutenant; Robert H. Ferguson, 2nd Lieutenant.

Roosevelt must have been close with these men, since they were frequent guests at Sagamore Hill functions after the war.

When soldiers departed from the lighthouse station, Scott would say, "Come again, come again. You soldier boys are always welcome to all I've got." Sometimes, he would add, "If I'd been ten years younger, I'd have gone myself!"[91]

In April of 1898, a U. S. Navy signal station was established at the Montauk Point Lighthouse, one of many such installations along the east coast of the United States. The equipment from the fog signal house was removed to make way for the naval militia corps. A signal pole was built on the property for use by the Coast Guard Service. In May, telephone service was installed, connecting with the life saving station at Quogue. In addition, nine homing pigeons from Newport, Rhode Island were added to the operation at the lighthouse.

In order to use the new signal pole, keepers had to learn an international code of signals to communicate with passing ships. However, for the duration of the war, the crew of the naval militia corps handled this responsibility at the lighthouse.[92]

Mounted men are seen riding at Camp Wikoff. The Dickinson House is right of center in the distance. (Theodore Roosevelt Collection, Harvard College Library, R560.3.EL61-106)

On August 25th, it was all business for the Rough Riders when a detachment of forty of them "invaded" East Hampton in search of several hundred horses which had run off from the camp. Members of the group "dashed along the roads and side lanes, scouring the country for the missing horses." The horses were thought to be "scattered along through Hither Woods, on Napeague Beach, and in the lanes around Amagansett, East Hampton and Wainscott, and it will be no easy task to gather them all in."[93]

Colonel Roosevelt managed to find time to gallop over the hills of Montauk every day, accompanied by his orderly, 24-year old Private Gordon Johnston. They usually wound up at the beach to watch the mighty waves pound the shore. The lure of the breakers attracted the Colonel to the point where on one occasion he shouted, "Bully! Perfectly Bully! I think I shall go in."

Private Johnston held Roosevelt's horse while Roosevelt prepared to enter the surf. As he stripped down he said to Johnston, "As soon as I come out after really dashing around in those breakers, I shall hold your horse and you can go in."

Johnston was perplexed. The water certainly looked inviting, but also rough, and it would not be military protocol to do so. While he mulled over the situation, he observed Roosevelt thoroughly enjoying

Circa 1898, this was probably how the Montauk Point Lighthouse appeared when Colonel Theodore Roosevelt and his entourage visited keeper James Scott on September 6, 1898. In this image, five individuals can be seen posing on the front porch of the keeper's dwelling. The building at right dates from 1838 and was formerly occupied by keepers before the house on the hill was constructed in 1860. (East Hampton Historical Society)

the experience of challenging one breaker after another. When the Colonel returned to the beach and redressed, he said to Johnston, "Now it's your turn, Johnston. I'll hold your horse."

Johnston replied, "It's absolutely unmilitary. It's impossible for a private to let a colonel hold his horse." But, at Roosevelt's insistence, Johnston went in.

Gordon Johnston (1874-1934) went on to become a lieutenant colonel and receive numerous honors in his military career, including the Congressional Medal of Honor, the Distinguished Service Medal, and the Distinguished Service Cross, but he never forgot that day with the Colonel on the beach at Montauk.[94]

The admiration, respect and appreciation for Colonel Roosevelt was never more poignantly displayed than on the afternoon of September 13, 1898 when his presence was requested by a group of officers to come to a location where 500 Rough Riders, 200 men of the Ninth and Tenth Cavalries, and a large number of visitors had already gathered. Roosevelt was presented with Frederick Remington's Bronco Buster statue as a profound indication of the love, admiration, and respect the Rough Riders had for their fearless leader.

Obviously moved by the gesture, Colonel Roosevelt spoke to his regiment for the final time:

Theodore Roosevelt and Gordon Johnston pause on a horseback jaunt to pose for a photographer at Camp Wikoff. (Theodore Roosevelt Collection, Harvard College Library, R560.3.EL61-025)

*It gives me extreme pleasure to look around among you and see men of every occupation, men of means and men who work with their hands for a livelihood, and at the same time know that I have you for friends. You are men of widely different pursuits, yet you stand here side-by-side, you fought shoulder-to-shoulder. No man asked quarter for himself, and each one went in to show that he was as good as his neighbor. That is the American spirit. You cannot imagine how proud I am of your friendship and regard.*[95]

The next day, per military custom, Roosevelt was the first officer to be mustered out of the service at Camp Wikoff.

On October 9, 1898, Secretary of War Russell Alger (1836-1907) ordered that the Seventh Infantry at Camp Wikoff be transferred, ending the military encampment.

Though the war was over and peace had returned, there were numerous allegations of poor planning and bureaucratic inefficiency that resulted in lack of adequate supplies for troops and the failure to contain the outbreak of diseases. These accusations of neglect were confirmed by the Dodge Commission, a body appointed by President McKinley and headed by Major General Grenville Dodge (1831-1916), a former Union officer in the Civil War. Under General Dodge, a War Investigation Commission began hearings in New York in October of testimony regarding the claims of abuse and mismanagement. The witnesses had been stationed at various locations, including Camp Wikoff, during the war.

Among those who testified was Colonel Roosevelt himself, who took the stand on November 22nd and spoke of the conditions he and his Rough Riders had experienced throughout the war. With regard to Camp Wikoff, he stated:

> *For the first three days a great deal of confusion prevailed, which I think was mostly unavoidable. For the first three days our sick and wounded didn't have cots. I did not think they were getting the attention they should be getting near a big city. After those first three days I have nothing to say, except that our regiment was admirably treated and our sick men were well treated. The records were badly kept at the camp, so that I sometimes couldn't find my own men, but so were the records of my own regiment, so I have no fault to find on that score. Men are more important than records, and if the men were well cared for that was all that concerned me. Again and again I would ask my men in the hospitals and would ask them how they were getting on, and they would say, 'Oh, this is heaven.'[96]*

Later, Roosevelt added:

> *They were getting chicken broth, they were getting milk. We got so much milk and goodies and things like that that we had to stop receiving them. I would take them around and give them to other regiments. My troop commanders and the regimental commanders who reported to me when I was brigade commander would report that they would not use any more delicacies; that they didn't want any more and could not use any more.[97]*

At the conclusion of the hearings, the War Commission filed its report on the overall effectiveness of the operation at Montauk Point:

> *Montauk Point was an ideal place for the isolation of troops who had been exposed to or had yellow fever, and for the recuperation of those greatly debilitated by malarial attacks of marked severity. The time allotted for preparation was altogether too short, and, as a consequence, the camp was occupied long before it was ready. Because of this and because of the great number of sick and convalescents and of those on the ground who were unconnected with the army, there was much confusion, some lack of proper attention to matters of sanitation and to the sick, and without doubt cases of distress…But, after all, there was much exaggeration in what was written and said about the conditions at Camp Wikoff- exaggeration at times intentional, generally with the result of unfamiliarity with the life of a soldier and with the appearance of a large number of sick and broken down men brought together in a limited space.[98]*

A significant segment of the forces that fought in Cuba were the Ninth and Tenth Regiments, referred to as the "colored" regiments. Described as "well-mannered, cheerful fellows," they "far sooner than any of the other Cuban veterans…recovered their spirits and vitality after the campaign." The consensus of opinion about their abilities on the battlefield was expressed by one who said, "those colored chaps fought like devils." Regarding the capture of San Juan Hill, the Ninth Regiment proved invaluable. The

Theodore Roosevelt is seen shaking hands with several unidentified troops at Camp Wikoff. The bronze statue, "The Bronco Buster," by Frederic Remington can be seen on the table next to Roosevelt. (Theodore Roosevelt Collection, Harvard College Library, R560.3.EL61-098a)

Rough Riders would not have held their position "but for the splendid charge of the black men to their support."[99] Colonel Roosevelt described them proudly in his farewell speech to the men at Camp Wikoff: "The Spaniards called them 'Smoked Yankees,' but we found them to be an excellent breed of Yankee."[100]

Of the nearly 30,000 troops that came to Camp Wikoff only 263 died; these men, according to Everett Rattray, were "lingering victims of tropical disease and tinned provisions, a scandal of the time, and some rest here still in unmarked graves near the [Montauk] Manor."[101]

The eventual removal of the dead to the Long Island Railroad for shipment to other cemeteries could not have been very pleasant, but on one occasion a touch of humor was added to the task, as related by Everett Rattray: A distant cousin, "celebrating the end of the Spanish-American War, is said to have fallen asleep up at the old [Montauk] Inn on Signal Hill and to have been nailed into a coffin by convivial friends. They carried him down to the station and shipped him west with a freight-car-load of dead Rough Riders. He revived at Long Island City,…made himself known, and was rescued, to be restored to the bosom of his long-suffering but patient family."[102]

The effects of having the thousands of sick and recovering troops camped on Montauk reached the members of the nearby Ditch Plains Life Saving Station. In mid October, life-saving station superintendent Arthur Dominy had completed a tour of all stations from Rockaway to Montauk and noticed that a few crew members were ill at the Ditch Plains station. One of them, David H. Miller, along with members of his family, was suffering from typhoid fever.[103]

An African American regiment (24th Infantry) marches into the Detention Camp at Camp Wikoff. (Theodore Roosevelt Collection, Harvard College Library, R560.3.EL61-113)

Of nearly 30,000 men sent to Montauk after the war, only 263 died from illnesses. The headstone of an infantryman named "Durand" is pictured in the foreground, in the cemetery at Camp Wikoff. (Theodore Roosevelt Collection, Harvard College Library, R560.3.EL61-124)

On December 6, 1898, Camp Wikoff was officially declared to be "no more." Although Montauk had returned to peacetime conditions, the virtues of using the area as a military stronghold continued. In September 1902 Montauk was "invaded." In a simulated exercise three "enemy" vessels entered Fort Pond Bay and succeeded in landing boats of troops in the old fishing village. A detachment took over the telegraph station, preventing the transmission of messages. In addition, ten boatloads of marines landed near the lighthouse property in order to attack and take over the signal stations at that locale. Reports indicated that there was "continued volleying in that direction, indicating that the Eleventh Battery of Fort Hamilton [in Brooklyn], which is encamped at Camp Carter, on the plains, two miles southeast of the Long Island Railroad station, is putting up a stiff resistance."[104]

Only about fifteen years later the clouds of war would again gather, and Montauk would become more than just a location for training exercises.

# CHAPTER 6

# World War I – Naval Aviation Station

As a way of preparing troops for war, on Saturday, June 21, 1913 cavalrymen from the New York National Guard went to Montauk for a nine day training session, "in a way that for thoroughness and practical details never has been experienced in the guard of any State." Under the direction of Major General John F. O'Ryan, a rigorous program was followed that included "practically continuous work during the hours of daylight, and after hours for guard duty." The training included the following programs:

> *Mounted work by squads under officers' leadership, school of the trooper, squad leading, marching on points, charging and rallying...troop and squadron in close and extended order...dismounted attack, fire discipline, fire control, 'to arms', disposition for defense of camp...mounted combat...field firing problems, both mounted and dismounted formations...all-day training in care of men and horses in the field...loading wagons and driving them, marching, making camp, preparing food, sanitation, bathing, care of feet... tactical rides or actual demonstration to illustrate such phases of cavalry field work as maneuvering over a rough country, passing defiles in vicinity of enemy...formation for advancing under artillery screen...swimming horses.*

It is not surprising that the cavalrymen "will not have to be sung to sleep."[105]

All dirigible submarine torpedoes used by the United States and manufactured in Brooklyn for the Navy were tested not far from Montauk at Noyack Bay (1891-1915) and Gardiner's Bay (from 1915). The home base for the testing fleet and mechanics' shop for assembling parts was at Long Wharf in Sag Harbor.

The E. W. Bliss Corporation made the first dirigible torpedoes (compressed air-propelled) in Brooklyn in 1891, where they were tested for flaws. Once cleared, they were sent to Sag Harbor. Over the years, the torpedo station there grew into a major industry for the quaint seaside village. During World War I the station was significantly enlarged. "One who visited Sag Harbor, at that time, found more than an hundred men handling the cigar-shaped cylindrical torpedoes."[106]

As the development of the range of dirigible torpedoes increased, it was found that the size of Noyack Bay was insufficient to accommodate far-ranging torpedoes. In 1915 operations shifted to Gardiner's Bay. In general, the waters of eastern Long Island were considered best for the testing of torpedoes. Though a torpedo testing range existed at Newport, Rhode Island, the majority of torpedoes that were sent to war ships, cruisers, and torpedo boats came from Sag Harbor.[107]

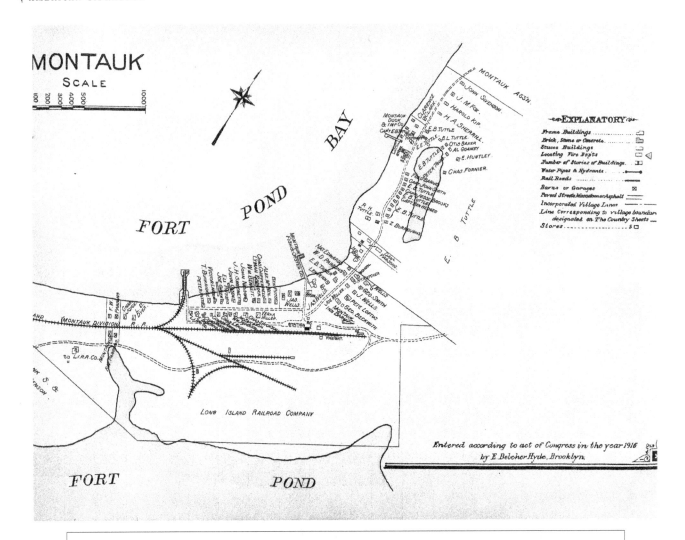

A map of old Montauk fishing village on Fort Pond Bay shows how the area looked in 1916. (Montauk Point Lighthouse Museum)

In March 1915 the Town of East Hampton proposed a plan to construct a cinder highway from where the existing Montauk Road ended at Cranberry Hill Road in Amagansett across Napeague to the western border of Montauk at the Nominicks hills. The following month it was reported that the "progressive spirit of East Hampton people is shown by the favorable vote to build a road across Napeague sand wastes to Montauk Highlands at a cost of $3,000."[108]

With world war on the horizon, in March 1917 reports were received regarding the presence of enemy submarines off Montauk Point. The Navy immediately sent destroyers and the Army sent airplanes to the area. An investigation revealed that the crafts were merely two patrol motor boats returning from a trial trip. The Navy claimed the incident "emphasizes the need for hydroaeroplanes for naval scouting purposes."[109]

War with Germany was formally declared on April 6, 1917. Two days earlier, Naval Base No. 4 was officially opened on Montauk under the leadership of Ensign W. A. Benjamin, who was replaced by Lt. Richard Welling on September 19, 1917. Montauk was selected as a training and enrollment camp for Eastern Long Island. Men between the ages of 18 and 58 who desired to join the service were sent here for examination, enrollment, and swearing in. The men stationed at Naval Base No. 4, at the Montauk and Shinnecock Lighthouses, and at eight Coast Guard stations between them, were employed mostly in "lookout" and guard duty. "Whatever sailed within sight of Montauk or Shinnecock Lights, including the fifty miles of coast between them, and whether on the surface of the sea, in the air, or in the waters below the surface, was promptly reported to headquarters and a close lookout systematically ordered at all the stations under control of Base No. 4."[110]

Former Montauk resident Edna Steck, who was about twelve when the base was built, recalled years later that a cinder road connected the base to the railroad and that roads were generally in poor condition until the arrival of the military.[111]

On April 21, 1917 a Naval Reserve enrollment center was set up at Amagansett. Here, men of East Hampton, Amagansett and Montauk took the oath of service in the Naval Reserve. In charge was Lt. R. B. Roosevelt.[112]

When war was declared, a YMCA War Work Headquarters was established for Long Island at Mineola. District Committees were set up in nearly every community. The one at East Hampton made certain that the men and officers stationed on Montauk were provided entertainment, as well as socks, sweaters, and other such items for their comfort. A YMCA hut was set up at Montauk Naval Base No. 4, which provided "frequent entertainments" to both Naval and Air Station personnel. The local women's committee of the YMCA made visits to Montauk bases, providing clothing and other necessities. A Soldiers' and Sailors' Club was established in the village of East Hampton.[113]

Dirigibles were photographed in a hangar at the Naval Air Station, Montauk, ca.1917. (Montauk Library)

Naval Air Station personnel are seen at work in the hangar at Montauk, ca.1917. (Montauk Point Lighthouse Museum)

On May 24, 1917 Secretary of War Newton Baker (1871-1937) issued an order declaring Montauk Point the location for the 19th and 20th Field Artillery.

On July 1, 1917 work began on a Naval Aviation Base at the Great Plain east of Fort Pond, Montauk, about where the current village is located. The flat open meadows made it useful as a landing field for dirigibles. Located on 33-acres, the base included a dirigible hangar (situated about where the Fisher Office Tower stands today), a seaplane hangar, barracks to accommodate 400 men, officer's quarters, machine shop, storerooms, hospital, photo laboratory, fabric shop, heating plant, a power plant, and other small structures. Planes based here patrolled the waters around eastern Long Island. Even the historic Second House was pressed into service for a time as a barracks for the crew that built the airfield.

The purpose of the station was to furnish an aerial patrol extending from the Fire Island Lighthouse to Nantucket Shoals and far enough at sea to cover the route of trans-Atlantic vessels.

Several hangars were built, the largest of which stood between the current Fisher Tower and the south shore of Fort Pond, "where my son has his garden center, and behind Luigi's Italian Restaurant," according to Montauk native Vinnie Grimes. The Pond was perfect for launching balloons, dirigibles, and hydroplanes under good weather conditions. The wireless station was taken over by the Government.

The dirigible hangar was enormous, with a base spanning 122-feet in length and the peak 85-feet high. The dirigible was inflated with hydrogen from a building that stood close by. The construction of a 75-foot runway enabled pilots to "run their machines almost into the house without much pushing, as the building is close to the water's edge of Fort Pond. It is anticipated that the facilities and natural advantages at hand here will make an excellent training camp."[114]

Construction moved swiftly along. The *East Hampton Star* noted: "The entire scene amazes one who has not visited Montauk within a month, and brings home the fact that Uncle Sam is going to prepare. All construction work is made of the strongest material and it is very evident that the camp will be a permanent one."[115]

In order to move equipment and supplies to the camp from the railroad station, plans were made to construct a concrete road from the station to the camp. A two mile road, now Edgemere Road, was soon built.

Lieutenant Marc A. Mitscher (1887-1947) was placed in charge of the newly-built station at Montauk. From sunup to sundown each plane at the base, armed with a machine gun and two bombs, took off from Fort Pond to fly a patrol mission. The air station was relatively quiet though. Mitscher made a patrol a few times a week. It was said that Lt. Mitscher "had more trouble with the crotchety spinster who managed the inn where the pilots lived than he did with U-boats. In spite of protests, she kept turning off the heat, until Mitscher stripped the furnaces of its valves."[116]

During Mitscher's time on Montauk, his wife, Frances, developed an interest in flying and accepted an invitation for a ride on a training blimp. Although she knew her husband was not pleased, she attempted to board the airship in secret. But Mitscher found out and, just before takeoff, told her, "Under no circumstances will you go up in that blimp."

Understandably, Frances was upset at missing this opportunity. But it turned out to be a blessing in disguise. As she and her husband watched the blimp climb higher and higher into the sky, "suddenly, control trouble developed and the blimp upended itself, to hang suspended for a few dangerous seconds. Mitscher pursed his lips and pointed a finger toward the odd position of the airship. Then he turned, to hide his laughter, and walked rapidly away."[117]

Lt. Mitscher would later rise to the rank of Admiral and serve valiantly during World War II.

Lieutenant Marc Mitscher (1887-1947) was placed in charge of the Naval Air Station on Montauk in 1917. Considered to be a quiet air station, it was not very challenging for Mitscher. He later became an Admiral and served valiantly during WWII.

The Naval Station faced only one major obstacle: Fort Pond, being fresh water and landlocked, froze over in winter, making landing of seaplanes impossible. However, the flat, open meadows to the east, made an excellent landing area for dirigibles year round.[118]

Between July 1917 and November 1918, 33-acres of the air base were developed including construction of hangars, barracks, shops, laboratories, a hospital, and other buildings. The winter of 1917 was severe, with December 8th being the last date for seaplanes to use Fort Pond for landings before the ice set in.

During that first winter, an appeal went out for warm clothing for the troops. The Comforts League Unit No. 1 of East Hampton responded with 42 sets of apparel. Each set consisted of a helmet, sweater, muffler, socks and wristlets. Summer residents who departed the East End in the fall were urged to send extra blankets and other items.[119]

With German U-boats sighted off the shores of Montauk, two companies of New York State Guards were formed.

During the war years, the Commissioner of Highways placed a sign at the beginning of the Montauk Road at the east end of Amagansett to deter civilian traffic:

WAR NOTICE!
PATRIOTIC CITIZENS WILL AVOID
USING THIS MONTAUK ROAD IF POSSIBLE.

At war's end, Lt. Welling wrote with pride regarding his men at Montauk:

*The men at Montauk Base 4, have worked and lived during the period of the war. Montauk and the experiences they went through there will always remain in their memory, and especially the aid and patriotic cooperation of their neighbors [in surrounding communities]…They can only look back on their part in the war, while at Montauk, with pleasure and satisfaction.*[120]

When hostilities ended, an inventory of the station revealed fifteen seaplanes, two dirigibles, and a kite balloon, along with 45 officers and 356 men, which was "a marked increase over the 58 officers and men who had 'pioneered' the establishment."[121]

Throughout its operation, the Montauk Naval Air Station had no reports of serious injuries, though several planes were partially or totally wrecked during operations. There were no problems, however, with the dirigibles.

It wasn't all work and no play at Montauk during the war. In early February 1918 a dance was held for the men at Majestic Hall in East Hampton. About forty men attended from the Air Station and the Naval Base at Montauk. With the participation of some twenty-five young ladies of the village, who acted as hostesses, the event was quite successful. Even men from Camp Upton at faraway Yaphank came to the party.[122]

There were other activities to entertain the men, one of which was noted by the *East Hampton Star* in the spring of 1918:

> *The entire camp wishes to express its appreciation of the piano donated by you folks, which arrived here a week ago. A good many of the boys play and the candidates for the camp quartet are almost as numerous as the pitchers we found here for our ball team…*

> *The [ball] team is called out for practice every evening now and there is some trouble in getting the men to keep away from the lure of fishing in Fort Pond. So far the catches have not amounted to anything and the fish caught are thrown back.*

> *Chief Storekeeper Ronne caught an eel the other evening. Perhaps we should have said that the eel caught Ronne, for a complete change of clothing was necessary after the Chief unhooked his catch.*[123]

The baseball team at Montauk participated in the "Long Island Naval Service Baseball League, Eastern Section." As reported in the *Suffolk County News* on July 12, 1918, team Montauk wasn't doing very well as seen in the standings to that point:

|                             | Won | Lost |
|-----------------------------|-----|------|
| Base No. 5 Sayville         | 4   | 1    |
| Base No. 3 Port Jefferson   | 3   | 3    |
| Naval Air Station, Montauk  | 1   | 2    |
| Radio Station, Sayville     | 1   | 3[124] |

In addition to the activity at the Naval Air Station, Coast Guard personnel served at stations on Montauk during the war. The following men were stationed at the Ditch Plains Station: Russell C. Miller (acting keeper), Noal H. Smith, Edward N. Payne, Russell C. Lester, Samuel B. Loper, Jr., Walter Lober, Stephen Raymond Conklin, Everett King, Albert Hand, and Owen Bennett. At the Hither Plain Station: Hiram F. King (keeper), Arthur G. Holliday, Charles G. Miller, Leonard A. Edwards, Cornelius Edgar Conklin, William S. Osborne, Floyd Bell, Frederick Beyers, George Sears.

At the Montauk Point Lighthouse, keeper John Miller indicated in a letter dated December 25, 1917 that there was a contingent of the "naval reserve force who are assigned here, which consists of five men."[125]

By mid-March 1918 it was reported that the Naval Air Station would continue as a training and experimental dirigible station, but would be abandoned as a seaplane base. About 100 men were to

An aerial view of the Montauk area shows the Naval Air Station. (Richard T. Gilmartin Collection, Montauk Point Lighthouse Museum)

remain to operate the station. By early July, only 50 men remained at the Montauk site, stirring rumors that the Naval Air Station was going to close.

On September 5th, a reception was held at the newly constructed YMCA hut at Montauk. Lt. Commander Richard Welling, U. S. Navy, who was in charge of the base, described the new facility as offering "the most desirable recreation…We have 'movie' exhibitions, delightful music, books and periodicals, and a committee of men take charge of matters of common interest in camp, including much that contributes to their efficiency."[126]

When war ended in November 1918, interest intensified as to who could fly the first biplane or dirigible non-stop across the Atlantic. The base at Montauk was still there, including abandoned biplanes and dirigibles. Wrote Dan Rattiner, "Somebody got an idea. Let's fly one of these things to Europe!"[127]

In February 1919 the first trial flight of the C-4 dirigible was made from Montauk. The airship went to Block Island, then back to Amagansett, and then returned to the air station. At the time it was considered the largest dirigible in the country, nearly 200-feet long, and could cruise for about 600 miles before having to land. About 220 men and 30 officers were stationed at the camp at that time, and it was expected that the Naval Air Station would be permanent, used as an experimental and Coast Guard station.[128]

On the morning of May 14, 1919, a C-5 dirigible, lead by Lieutenant Commander E. W. Coil, took off, aided by a strong wind from the west. It was a gallant effort, but one doomed to failure. It safely reached St. Johns, Newfoundland. After replenishing needed supplies it prepared to take off. However, a storm with wind gusts of sixty miles per hour battered the ship. What followed resembled a scene from a cartoon adventure:

*The ship was picked up like a child's toy and smashed down, breaking a propeller and damaging the control car. At that moment a strong gust hit the ship, shooting it into the air. [R. A. D.] Preston [a member of the ground crew], afraid that the crew would be carried away, shouted to let go. The ground crew obeyed just as the two officers jumped...The crewless C-5 leaped high in the air and started across the Atlantic...it was never seen again. If the ship had been manned, it very likely would have been the first aircraft ever to cross an ocean.*[129]

After about a year of rumors about the future of the base, the Montauk Naval Air Station officially shut down on August 5, 1919. The camp, which cost several million dollars to construct, was to be sold privately or torn down. By December, the Lewis Wrecking Company was selected to demolish the 50-odd wooden buildings, and I. Y. Halsey of East Hampton dismantled the seaplane hangar and attached it to his garage in East Hampton, which would "add about 1000 square feet of floor space to his establishment, thus placing it in the lead of any other garage on the east end of Long Island."[130]

The remaining twenty-one sailors, basically on guard detail, were apparently so content with their surroundings that if they could "persuade the Secretary of the Navy, would prefer to remain for the rest of their lives." According to one sailor, Joseph Shapiro, "I have sailed the seven seas...I've barked my shins in Shanghai and beached my boat on the Barbary Coast, but you can take it from me that this is the snuggest little berth I've ever hung my hammock in."[131]

According to the *New York Times*:

*When these men finally left this Montauk paradise, they "must forego frequent feasts in millionaire's homes, automobiles at their disposal, seaplanes at their call for a hurried visit to Manhattan, duck hunting, fishing, and shooting, not to mention invitations to parties from the girls roundabout Amagansett, East Hampton, and Sag Harbor. In no naval station in the world, perhaps, is life made so attractive as in the United States Naval Air Station at Montauk. Duties are nominal; pleasures are phenomenal.*[132]

It was apparent by January 1920 that the Naval Air Station was preparing to shut down, as security became noticeably relaxed when compared to the war years. The *East Hampton Star* reported just how relaxed the operation had become in describing how a visitor was received at that time:

*If your credentials were O. K. you were allowed to go about your business. Everything in those days was hustle and bustle at the camp. Those were war days. Today everything is changed. You are allowed to wander into the camp from any side, and look about as much as you please. After walking about the camp and making an inspection without interruption, if you are in search of the commander, you will probably eventually run into the officers' headquarters building, not by any given direction or order by a guard but more by good luck than anything else.*

*You wander through the kitchen, where you are confronted by no less a personage that Jos. Shapiro, head of the commissary department... If he considers everything satisfactory and you wish to see the commander he announces your presence to Lieut. Evans.*[133]

At that time, representatives from the Lewis Wrecking Company were there to inventory the buildings and their contents.

In March 1920 dismantling of the huge hangar was begun by 30 mechanics from the Bethlehem Steel works, who attached the building onto another hangar situated at Cape May, New Jersey, making it one of the largest dirigible hangars in the United States. The new structure was 708-feet long and 200-feet high.[134]

A notable structure at the Air Station was the bomb house, used to house tons of high explosives and depth bombs. The building, standing on the edge of Fort Pond, was built of solid concrete, with walls of reinforced concrete 14-inches thick. Though weighing hundreds of tons, the Lewis Wrecking Company completely demolished the structure in just three days in May 1920.[135] The entire base was leveled that month.

By August 1920, Fort Pond was the scene of battleships and seaplanes conducting maneuvers. The battleships were the *Pennsylvania* (flagship), *Nevada, Arizona, Utah, Florida,* and *North Dakota.* The seaplanes came from Cape May and stayed several weeks for tactical purposes.[136] In succeeding years, almost every summer the Navy conducted target practice in Gardiner's Bay.

# CHAPTER 7

# Camp Welsh 1922 – 1924

IN MAY 1921 it was announced that National Guard camps would be established on Montauk during the summer of 1922. Meanwhile, members of the Sixth and Seventh Field Artillery units arrived in mid June to stay for six to eight weeks at an installation known as Camp Welsh. Members of the New York and New Jersey National Guard arrived from late June through August.

At that time it was reported that the reverberation of guns fired by the artillery units at Montauk could be felt as far as fifty miles away. An estimated 4,000 artillerymen and cavalrymen filled the camp. Many visitors came to Montauk to observe the activities.[137]

Though the camp appeared to have a successful season, there were doubts that it would continue. First, there were some on Montauk who complained about the camp's presence. In addition, according to Long Island Congressman Frederick Cocks Hicks (1872-1925), in February 1922, since the camp was not government owned, it appeared doubtful that the necessary tract of land at Montauk for camp use could be secured. Hicks also claimed that it was "not contemplated that any funds will be available for the improvement of roads leading to this camp as there is no intention of maintaining it as a permanent center."[138]

The road Hicks referred to was the Montauk Road, which was then unpaved from the east end of Amagansett all the way to Montauk Point.

However, there were those who favored Camp Welsh. There were businessmen at Montauk, as well as at the east end communities of Sag Harbor, East Hampton and Amagansett, who were nothing short of delighted at its presence.

In April 1922, a decision was reached by the Army administrative center at Governor's Island, New York City, selecting Montauk as the site for a field artillery camp in connection with the Citizen's Military Training Camps. Groups of instructors visited all the high schools in the corps area to explain the advantages which the training camps offered to young men. With the use of Montauk as an instruction camp, efforts were made to develop a paved road across Napeague to Montauk.[139] In early May, Army officers journeyed to Montauk to survey a possible camp site on the east side of Fort Pond. Meanwhile, some army officers conducted preliminary surveys for a road across Napeague. The *East Hampton Star* reported, "From this fact it might be inferred that the War Department realizes that something will have to be done on this road if a permanent camp is to be maintained at Montauk."[140]

No record exists of any highway being formally laid out across Montauk before the year 1900. It wasn't until the creation of the Naval Air Station that land was acquired for what would become the Montauk Highway we know today.

On August 2, 1922 it was announced that five citizen's military training camps in the Second Corps

Sunrise Trail over Hither Hills    Montauk, Long Island, N. Y.

In the mid 1920s efforts were made to build a concrete road across Napeague to Montauk, most likely due to increased use of an old cinder road by military personnel. By the late 1920s a highway ran from Amagansett to Montauk. This view shows the Old Montauk Highway in Hither Hills, Montauk. (Montauk Point Lighthouse Museum)

area were opened for a thirty-day training period. The infantry camp was at Plattsburgh, New York, cavalry and engineer camps at Camp Dix, New Jersey, the Signal Corps at Camp Vail, New Jersey, coastal artillery at Fort Hancock, New Jersey, and the field artillery at Montauk. Seven hundred candidates attending the Citizens Military Training Camp at Camp Welsh, Montauk were transported by rail from Pennsylvania Station in New York. This unit, under the jurisdiction of the Second Corps Area Headquarters at Governors Island, was made up of citizens from Delaware, New Jersey and New York. A total of about 1,800 U. S. Army Regulars were stationed at the camp in Montauk during the course of the summer. On July 30, 1922 members of the 102nd Ammunition Train National Guard and the 104th Field Artillery National Guard went to Montauk and remained there until August 13th. The 104th unit "will take along horses, guns, and various other equipment, which will require fifty-two railroad freight cars to handle."[141]

On August 13th members of the 105th Field Artillery National Guard and 132nd Ammunition Train National Guard—about 2,800 men—went to train until August 27th.

It seems that the men who camped on Montauk were so greatly enamored of the place that they recommended it becoming a permanent training and camping station, since the "sand dunes, the hills and the ocean provide a tonic which is exhilarating to the body as well as to the mind".[142]

Between 1921-1923 thousands of soldiers from Regular Army, National Guard, and Citizen Military Training Corps Field Artillery units trained at Montauk. A campsite just east of Fort Pond Bay known as Camp Welsh was selected to accommodate training personnel.

Probably due to increasing use of the cinder road, it was decided to concrete the road from Amagansett to the Montauk boundary at Nominicks. What really made it necessary was that by 1922 the military encampment at Montauk would need to transport heavy army trucks over the road, and the cinder road would be incapable of handling the heavy loads.[143]

By October of 1922 East Hampton Town highway officials were complaining about the damage done to the cinder road by the many army trucks and gun carriages going to and from the artillery camp on Montauk. As reported by the *Suffolk County News:*

> *The Napeague road has been cut through in 40 or more places and during the summer has been damaged several thousand dollars worth. While the Army was using the road Army officers were on the job to keep it in repair, but as soon as the soldiers left the camp, the repair work ceased. The holes are still there, however.*[144]

Fort Pond with Camp Welsh on east side is shown in 1922. Second House is visible at left. (Courtesy of the Queens Borough Public Library, Long Island Division, Eugene L. Armbruster Photographs)

Repair work was scheduled to begin in the spring of 1923. Town officials felt that they had had a "poor deal" from Federal authorities regarding the repairs caused by the military vehicles and equipment.[145] The newly-paved road was not concreted until 1927.

During August 1922 it was learned that there were numerous cases of theft at Camp Welsh, including personal property of Regular Army Officers. Following an investigation it was determined that Jessie James, a discharged soldier, had removed a "trunkful of officer's clothing" from camp and kept it at a boarding house in East Hampton. He was sentenced to 60-days in jail at Riverhead, Long Island. There also were reports that "several thousand dollars worth of equipment was stolen and disposed of for money and liquor."[146]

During August 1922 field artillery practice was held near Great Pond, after horses were first removed to a safer place. Targets were arranged at a distance of 1,800 to 3,200 yards. The firing:

> *was across open country with many hills and hallows between gun position and target. In the afternoon the firing was across Great Pond at targets situated upon Prospect Hill, which has an elevation of about 165 feet, while the gun positions were close to sea level. The range was between three and four thousand yards.*

> *The firing was with shrapnel, therefore it was the aim of each officer firing to place his cone of fire wherein it would do the most damage. As soon as this was arrived at by corrections, the battery was ready to 'fire for effect.' The accuracy of his observations was determined by the minimum number of shots fired to obtain this result.*

At the conclusion, officers in charge expressed their approval with the effectiveness of the practice and conduct of the men involved.[147]

Dick White recalled the following about Camp Welsh:

> *They held gunnery practice at the camp. They had cannons on what is now the ball field [Hank Zebrowski Field on Edgemere Lane] and they would fire canisters over the hills toward the harbor. You have to remember there was nobody in the harbor area at that time. You can go there today and see holes in the ground and there are mini balls all around.*

> *There are three or four houses along Edgemere Road that were officers' houses. They are very much the same in appearance. The bivouac area was where Suffolk County National Bank, the bakery and the stores are.*[148]

After a few years of operation at Montauk, Camp Welsh was discontinued. In May 1924 it was announced that the Montauk Company, which was established by Long Island Railroad President Austin Corbin in 1895, was considering the sale of property. In August, Robert Moses, chairman of the Long Island State Parks Commission, acquired about 1,700 acres of Montauk lands via eminent domain for development as Hither Hills and Montauk Point State Parks. Then, in 1925, millionaire entrepreneur Carl Fisher bought virtually the rest of Montauk for about $2.5 million dollars to develop as another Miami Beach. Thus ended further military use of Montauk lands for the time being.

In January 1931 Congressman Frederick A. Britten (1871-1946), Chairman of the House Commission on Naval Affairs, asked for the cooperation of the Long Island Chamber of Commerce in preparing for the operations of the Navy's Scouting Fleet from Fort Pond Bay, Montauk in the coming summer months. Maneuvers in the Long Island/Narragansett area would have a base in a Long Island harbor. The Fleet consisted of approximately twenty-five destroyers, ten cruisers, two battleships, and an aircraft carrier. Personnel totaled about 7,000.

Camp Welsh, Montauk, is pictured in 1922. (Courtesy of the Queens Borough Public Library, Long Island Division, Eugene L. Armbruster Photographs)

A 1922 image shows soldiers from Camp Welsh and a boy with army truck near Parsons Inn, Montauk. (Courtesy of the Queens Borough Public Library, Long Island Division, Eugene L. Armbruster Photographs)

There was high praise for the quality of Fort Pond Bay to handle such a volume of vessels without congestion. Robert Moses made plans to accommodate both sailors and visitors at nearby Hither Hills and Montauk Point State Parks.[149]

In mid-August, 27 warships carrying 5,000 officers and men of the Atlantic scouting fleet left Newport, Rhode Island for Montauk in miserable weather. Congressman Britton and his friend, entrepreneur Carl Fisher, were among those ready to welcome the fleet at Montauk. Plans were in place to entertain the men at parties in the Hamptons. Even a carnival at Patchogue some 70 miles away was arranged. To Congressman Britton, "everything looked bright except the weather."[150]

That is when troubles began. No sooner did the fleet anchor at Fort Pond Bay, when:

*Seaman Francis Barnes fell overboard from a ship's boat and was drowned. Next day it rained hard. Grumblings began to be heard...there was nothing to do in Montauk, nothing to look at but the fishermen's cottages and the hotel, at which prices were too high even for captains; rain kept all but a few sailors from the carnival at Patchogue... The complaints grew louder.[151]*

Britten intended to promote Montauk as a permanent summer base, which prompted strong protests from authorities at Newport. Britton had a quick response for the "bejeweled dowagers and debutantes" of the famed city of the Gilded Age: "this is the United States Navy and not the Newport Navy."[152]

The government-built road (now Edgemere Street) between Montauk station and Camp Welsh, Montauk, was built 1917-18. This image was taken in 1923. Fort Pond is in the distance. (Courtesy of the Queens Borough Public Library, Long IslandDivision, Eugene L. Armbruster Photographs)

Once the weather improved the sailors went ashore for their athletic tournament. Alas, there were more problems:

> Crowds of them flocked to the bus station, waited for busses to take them to the fields. No busses came. Finally appeared Promoter Snyder, acting secretary of the bus line, to explain that the line had lost $1000 in two days because nobody used it, so the busses rolled out of town. Sailors piled in taxi cabs, paid as high as $1.25 a mile. As the week wore on the social columns carried more and more news of teas, dinners, receptions, dances for the officers. Long Island hostesses were pleased- until an enterprising newshawk discovered the fact that so few officers had volunteered to attend the social affairs to which they had been invited that the commanding officers had to pick out the required number of guests and order them to go.[153]

When the naval maneuvers were completed, Congressman Britten declared them to be a complete success and claimed the servicemen enjoyed their time at Montauk. He emphasized the value of Fort Pond Bay as a harbor and the recreational possibilities there. However, due to Britten being a close friend of Carl Fisher, who was suffering through financial woes at the time at Montauk, there were those who saw a case of *quid pro quo* on Britten's part to bring increased activity to Fisher's failed Montauk project of the 1920s. When servicemen were asked about their experience they "found little of recreational interest at Montauk and many of the officers said the place was inaccessible and expensive."[154]

# CHAPTER 8

# World War II

## Naval Torpedo Testing Range

ON SEPTEMBER 1, 1939, Germany, under the rule of Adolph Hitler and the Nazis, invaded Poland, touching off World War II. Although the United States did not enter the war for more than two years, efforts were made to protect and defend our coastlines. A part of the defense effort was announced in January 1940 when plans were made for four air bases along the East Coast from Massachusetts to Puerto Rico, including an aviation station at Floyd Bennett Field in Brooklyn. At that time, Montauk Point was considered as a site for an air base, but rejected because of "cost and convenience."[155]

In March 1940 the Coast Guard emphasized the importance of safety along our shores by setting up an exhibit entitled "Safety at Sea" at the New York World's Fair in Flushing, New York. In addition to displays depicting the duties and activities of Coast Guard personnel, a forty-foot model of the Montauk Point Lighthouse was included, "complete with flashing lights."[156]

During the war, the East Coast was threatened by the presence of German submarines (U-boats). In the Northeast the danger of attacks on the major cities of New York and Boston made eastern Long Island, particularly Montauk, a likely invasion point. Eventually, with the Army, Navy and Coast Guard having operations there, the entire facility was officially called a "US Military Reservation." However, local residents simply referred to it as "Camp Hero." Part of the plans for Montauk involved the takeover of the old fishing village on Fort Pond Bay.

The fishing village had its origins in the 1880s and, with the arrival of the Long Island Railroad in 1895, it soon became a bustling town, especially following the departure of troops stationed on Montauk after the Spanish American War. During the summer of 1899 a group of fishermen arrived from Nova Scotia and settled at Fort Pond Bay, occupying previously abandoned buildings. Additional dwellings were soon constructed.

Life was different in the old fishing village. In a 1998 interview, Miriam Byrnes said, "We used to pick the coal to use in our stoves off the railroad. Some of the engineers would throw it overboard…We ran out of fuel while it's cookin', we'd have to stop and run across the tracks and pick up coal, go home again…we was primitive…very primitive."[157]

During the Great Depression, when many communities suffered, the little village on the bay thrived through fishing and bootleg liquor. Wrote Dan Rattiner, "This remote village of about 300 residents could have paved its streets with gold from the shower of money that came its way because of rumrunning."[158] The great hurricane of September 21, 1938 moved most of the buildings off their foundations, destroying many, and it was the end of 1939 until everything was rebuilt and repaired.

On January 14, 1942 the Panamanian tanker *Norness* was torpedoed by a German U-boat about 60-miles southeast of Montauk Point. Fortunately, all aboard were safely rescued in lifeboats. The sinking ship sent patches of oil onto the beaches of East Hampton Town. The Coast Guard conducted beach patrols. Unauthorized civilians were prohibited from going near the Montauk Point Lighthouse.

What the hurricane didn't remove of the old fishing village, the U. S. Navy did; the small homes and businesses "sheathed in fish-box lumber and built to multiples of this measure long before most architects had heard the word 'module'".[159] A few old structures remain today.

An aerial view shows old Montauk fishing village in the 1930s. The hurricane of September 21, 1938 destroyed much of the village, and the Navy removed the rest in the early 1940s for construction of a torpedo testing range. (East Hampton Historical Society)

In the 1930s, a little country road led into Montauk's old fishing village. The sign on the right advertises "Full Course Dinner 60c." The quaint little community was totally gone by 1943 when the Navy established their torpedo testing range at Fort Pond Bay. (East Hampton Historical Society)

Not long after the U. S. entered World War II, Fort Pond Bay was selected as a torpedo testing site for the Navy. Wrote Dan Rattiner: "It was easy enough to lease the property from the railroad—not only the tracks and the station and the docks and all the land in between—and it was also easy to bulldoze down all the fishermen's houses that had been built there illegally. There was an outcry, but it did no good."[160]

The bay attracted the Navy and in 1942 the village was torn down for construction of a Navy torpedo testing base. Some forty dwellings were bulldozed, including the general store, a restaurant, a fishing station, and the post office. The Montauk School was saved, moved by the Navy to a site along Industrial Road just west of where the railroad tracks now cross the road.

According to Montauk resident Gene Beckwith Jr., the residents of the old fishing village were given two options by the Navy: move your home or abandon it. If you chose to leave your home you were given $300 to establish a residence elsewhere. Beckwith participated in the famous D-Day invasion of Normandy and later in the invasion of Okinawa.[161]

One notable structure from the old village was the Trail's End Restaurant. Steeped in history from the days of Prohibition this landmark, which held the oldest liquor license in Montauk, was moved to its present location on Edgemere Road in the new village.

In March 1942 plans were announced for the construction of a Navy auxiliary base on Star Island, Montauk. Barracks, wharfs, and other buildings costing $80,000 were part of the plans. The site was once the location of the infamous Star Island Casino, a gambling resort constructed in 1929 by Carl Fisher, catering to the wealthy. It was subject to numerous raids by police during the wild days of Prohibition.

Montauk Manor was used as a barracks for GI's, the Long Island Railroad station as the main gate house, and the Fisher Office Tower as officer's quarters. Additional dormitories were built nearby. Even the old Surf Club on the ocean was occupied by the military. Men who were not drafted into the service were put to work building defense installations at Montauk.

The Montauk Manor was built and opened by Carl Fisher in 1927 as part of his plan to make Montauk a playground for the well-to-do. It saw service as a barracks during WWII, housing military personnel from the nearby torpedo testing range at Fort Pond Bay. It is seen here in 1954. (Richard T. Gilmartin Collection, Montauk Point Lighthouse Museum)

The Naval Torpedo Testing Range at Montauk was officially commissioned on March 25, 1943. Guy C. Hitchcock, Captain, U. S. Navy was the commanding officer for the duration of the range's existence. The naval section base on Star Island was then discontinued; its buildings and dock taken over by the Torpedo Testing Range.

The seaplane hangar and ramp were built on the west side of Fort Pond Bay. Facilities for the range were established along the south and east sides of the bay, the former location of the old Montauk fishing village. The old Long Island Railroad station became the main gate house for the base.

On August 30, 1943 the first of 196 aircraft torpedo drops was made from a plane east of Gardiner's Island. Each torpedo was followed by an observation plane until it was retrieved by a boat.

If any torpedoes needed repair they were taken to a windowless one-story structure known as an overhaul shop at the base. It should be noted that the naval base at Montauk was the only torpedo range not manned with civilian personnel.

With the creation of the torpedo testing range, came restrictions to vessels plying the waters of Block Island Sound and Fort Pond Bay, as reported in the *East Hampton Star* on May 6, 1943:

> [N]o vessel shall enter or navigate that part of the restricted area in Fort Pond Bay, from Culloden Point to Rocky Point, except commercial craft may enter from or depart to the eastward by navigating close to the shore line, but shall not navigate westward of 'Duryea's Wharf'. Such navigation will proceed at its own risk. All other waters of the restricted area shall be open to navigation except at such times as the torpedo testing range is in actual operation. When the range is in operation all traffic is prohibited, except for craft navigating close to the shore line and not west of Duryea's.[162]

The *East Hampton Star* described the testing of the "tin fish" in February 1944:

> Shot from a surface vessel or dropped from a flying boat, the torpedoes must measure up to high standards as they churn the water for miles over the Navy's ranges. If they don't stay on the line or travel at the right speed or remain at the right depth or go the correct distance, they are overhauled and tested again. Sometimes it's a case of test-firing them over and over again…

> Out in Fort Pond Bay…is anchored the 1,500-ton four-deck craft around which the work of the station evolves…It is called a barge and its official Navy designation is a YTT. From it are launched the 'no-man subs' for their test runs. Two types of torpedoes are tested at Montauk, one for use by surface vessels such as destroyers and the other for planes. Every 'tin fish' sent to Montauk is fired at least once from the YTT…

> There's never a dull moment on the range while firing is in progress…Some [torpedoes] go ashore, and men instantly go after them. Some sink, and the spot is marked so that divers may be sent down to retrieve them…Some torpedoes, improperly adjusted, are surface runners. They slam down the range kicking up bursts of spray as their twin propellers, whirling in opposite directions, whip the water into foam. These surface runners, if they get off the beam, are dangerous. Only recently one smashed through the sides of a range boat.[163]

On July 1, 1944 the use of a blimp began at the range. It operated from Fisher's Island where mooring masts were provided. It also helped in the recovery of torpedoes.

Dick White recalled:

*I remember seeing the use of dirigibles, especially in the summer. They were used to spot submarines because of their slow movement. I remember them dropping ropes down and people on the beach holding them there. I guess they were trying to stay in one spot.*

*I remember walking out to see Walter Gray, who was the caretaker of the Church Estate, which is located down Ranch Road behind the stables on the beach. I recall walking along the beach, and there used to be a tower on the beach at Ditch Plains, and there would be a Coast Guardsman in the tower with a megaphone. He would yell down, 'Halt! Who goes there?'" My father would say he was Franklin Delano Roosevelt, and the guy in the tower would say, 'Proceed, Mr. President,' and he would walk down the beach.*

*Montauk was a very small place and my dad owned the drug store, so if you wanted cigarettes or an ice cream soda or things of that nature, we had the store for it. There were only about 500 people living in Montauk in those days, so you knew everybody.*

Edna Steck recalled Navy men marching to military music down the hill at Montauk Manor at various times of the day, along with airplane spotters located in a building near the schoolhouse. She remembered shows put on by the U. S. O. in the Carl Fisher tennis courts building. They were open to the locals as well as servicemen.[164] Another resident, Elizabeth Job, recalled working with fellow teenagers as airplane spotters at the Montauk School. She also noted that a U. S. O. canteen was held in the basement of St. Therese's Catholic Church in town.[165]

Vincent (Vinnie) Grimes was born on Montauk on September 17, 1928 and has called it home his entire life. In an October 2009 interview with the author at Grimes' home in the Shepherd's Neck section of Montauk, he recalled the days when his town was abuzz with activity at the torpedo testing range and elsewhere:

*When the Navy came in, they gave you so much time to move your house away. If you didn't they'd give you $250 and bulldoze it. In the old days the houses were owned by the people that built them. They were mainly Canadians who were pretty up to putting in the foundation and building the houses. Not like today where you need a mason, a shingler, a finisher inside the house, a roofer. In those days they would do everything.*

*My mother was from Prince Edward Island. They moved here mainly to fish. My father was from Edmonton, and he came here with Carl Fisher around 1926.*

*We had been at peace long enough [since World War I]. We let our armaments go to hell. Nobody thought we were gonna go to war again. At the torpedo testing range they used to fire them from a PT boat tied at the dock. They had no warheads. When those torpedoes went crazy the sirens would go off. The seaplane would take off, the PT boat would run out, they'd drop a marker where the thing went down, and send a diver down to bring it up. Sperry Gyroscope came out and finally straightened out the problem so the torpedoes would run straight.*

*Some of those torpedoes would boomerang; go up the bank, smash up the docks, go everywhere! One landed in the back of a guy's pickup truck. The guy was a lobsterman and a pretty good drinker, and when he got up next morning and checked the back of his pickup, he went back inside and asked his wife, "Was I carrying a load last night?" His wife said yeh he was pretty drunk. He said, "I don't know where I picked this thing up!"*

*At the base the military kept the track and the old railroad station and built a new one for us next to it. They needed the track to bring their heavy equipment down there to Fort Pond Bay. The military used this station to ship guys out here....*

A proud lifelong Montauk resident, Vinnie Grimes is pictured in 2009. He and his family are distinct threads in the fabric of Montauk history. His stories of old Montauk are fascinating and exciting, and at times mischievously sprinkled with a sparkling sense of humor. (Author photo)

*It was nothing for us to have caravans of military trucks and so forth going through Montauk all the time.*

*You doubled up on your houses. My grandmother and grandfather moved in with my mother and dad and rented their house to Navy personnel. The Playhouse was used for movies and boxing bouts.*

*The whole military operation would use the local school buses to take the guys to the movies in East Hampton and pick 'em up when the movies were over and bring 'em back home. When I was in high school we'd take the bus with the sailors who were going to the movies. The bus driver was the driver from here. That was an experience! We didn't drink, but these guys'd get on there at night drunk as skunks, heave all over the place.*

*The Navy built Navy Road. They had water towers up there, and they had bunkers up there with ammunition. Off the road was a hangar for the seaplane and a dock for PT boats.*

*A lot of those guys stayed here or married girls from here and moved away. In those days we were a close knit community and related to each other. That's why I had to go to the Bronx and get a wife, 'cause I was related to all the girls out here; they were my cousins!*[166]

In October 1944 a Columbus Day Dance was held at the Montauk U.S.O. at which awards were presented to volunteers from East Hampton, Amagansett and Montauk who had served more than 50 hours. From Montauk, the Junior Hostesses were: "Misses" Mary Ellen Belber, Ruth Cook, Betty Darenberg, Eva McDonald, Pat McDonald, Kerstin Olsen, Viola Olsen, Betty Pfund, Grace Pospisil, Margaret Pugh, Marion Walker, and Mrs. Elizabeth Lane. The Senior Hostesses were: Mrs. Edward Baker, Mrs. Theodore Cook, Mrs. Carl Darenberg, Mrs. Carleton Farrell, Mrs. William Lyke, Mrs. Leonard McDonald, Mrs. Joseph Miller, Mrs. Ruth Miller, Mrs. Louis McDonald, Mrs. Olgot Olsen, Mrs. William Parsons, Mrs. Chris Pfund, Mrs. Fred Pitts, Mrs. Arthur Sewell, Mrs. Charles Tuma, Mrs. Richard White and Mrs. Ed Pospisil.[167]

In August 1944 the Bureau of Ordnance announced plans to close down the base and move operations to the Naval Torpedo Station at Newport, Rhode Island. On December 7, 1944 all equipment and personnel were transferred to Newport.

With the official closing of the station, on February 28, 1945, the Montauk U.S.O. also shut down after sixteen months of service. However, its local women volunteers realized the importance of service to the smaller groups that remained. Lt. John B. Hambrick, Commanding Officer, said that a recreation center was being remodeled at the base which would be used by various military units and indicated that the "volunteers can be of great service to us in acting as senior hostesses at our dances and assisting us in the recruiting of the junior hostesses. We wish to maintain the same high standards in the selection of hostesses that was maintained at the USO...We deeply appreciate this offer by the volunteers of Montauk and East Hampton to be of assistance."[168]

The station was officially disestablished on March 1, 1945. In April, a number of the buildings at the naval base were sold by sealed bids. Sales were on an all-cash basis and bids had to be accompanied by a deposit of at least ten percent of the value of the item. Among the properties offered:

*–One-story frame building 80' x 20' used at Boatswain's Shop*
*–three paint storehouses 35' x 18', 24' x 14', and 20' x 20'*
*–storehouse 24' x 12'*
*–sentry house 14' x 12'*

—*oil storehouse 21' x 8'*
—*blacksmith shop with forge 16' x 14'*
—*dispensary, dispensary garage, dispensary storehouse, and dispensary emergency lighting building*
—*two sentry houses*
—*athletic gear locker 16' x 14'*
—*two story barracks building 218' x 36'*[169]

After the war, some of the Navy buildings were used by the New York Ocean Science Laboratory. Other buildings and the dock were taken over for recreational use. Among the new establishments was the Fish Shangri-la which was popular for a few years at Fort Pond Bay. The old torpedo testing station was torn down in the mid 1980s; the site is now occupied by a condominium development called Roughrider's Landing. A lasting memory of the old village is a scale model of it on display at the East Hampton Town Marine Museum on Bluff Road in Amagansett.

## Montauk Point Lighthouse

Amid the hustle and bustle around Montauk, there were signs of an eventual takeover by the military at the Montauk Point Lighthouse, as evidenced by log entries from head lighthouse keeper Thomas A. Buckridge:

| | |
|---|---|
| 1/21/41 | airplane maneuvers all crew on watch for planes |
| 5/3/41 | Lt. Col. Bray here with a detail |
| 6/6/41 | Detail from Fort Michie here for gun practice |
| 6/7/41 | Coast artillery practically in charge |
| 6/9/41 | Army occupying everything |
| 6/11/41 | 242 coast artillery from Fort Michie encamped here for gun practice |
| 12/9/41 | standing airplane watch, air-plane scare in New York |
| | [this was two days after the Japanese attack on Pearl Harbor] |
| 1/24/42 | Coast Guard started first watch at 4pm |
| 1/25/42 | Standing double watch. Coast Guard in tower, keepers on ground |
| 6/13/42 | Called entire crew to patrol shore |
| | [this was in response to word that Germans had landed at Amagansett] |
| 8/14/42 | Changed light from 1000 kw to 100 kw[170] |

By January of 1942 the families of the lighthouse keepers had to move off the property because of the war. Second Assistant Keeper George Warrington's family relocated to a rented cottage in the Shepherd's Neck section of Montauk, while First Assistant Keeper Jack Miller's family returned to Springs near East Hampton. Head keeper Thomas Buckridge's wife returned to Essex, Connecticut while he was reassigned to the Saybrook Breakwater Lighthouse in early 1943.[171]

To improve communications as part of military surveillance at the lighthouse, the Coast Guard installed a telephone in the watch deck room of the tower in January 1942. By this time the Coast Guard had taken over watches at the station.

In keeping with the role of surveillance, a change had to be made in the appearance of the brightly shining tower beacon. On July 1, 1940 the lighthouse tower was electrified and a 1000-watt incandescent

Lighthouse keeper Thomas Buckridge, left, poses with assistant keepers Jack Miller, center, and George Washington Warrington at Montauk Lighthouse in 1942. They were the last civilian keepers to maintain the light until the Army took over the property in 1943. (Montauk Point Lighthouse Museum)

George Warrington, 2$^{nd}$ assistant keeper, poses in a seemingly pensive mood while keeping warm at Montauk Point Lighthouse, ca.1938. (Montauk Point Lighthouse Museum)

electric bulb was installed, sending a beam of light 19 nautical miles (22 statute miles) out to sea. However, this light, so helpful to ships in peacetime, was now aiding Nazi submarines by silhouetting allied vessels as they sailed by Montauk Point. Therefore, on August 14, 1942 the 1000-watt bulb was replaced by one a mere 100-watts, causing a noticeable decrease in the sinking of allied vessels in the area.

Regular lightkeeper's logbook entries ended on April 30, 1943 with the departure of the civilian keepers and the Army in complete control of the lighthouse. Coast Guard occupation of the lighthouse station did not take place until late 1946.

The keeper's dwelling underwent several changes. Instead of three families, an average of ten Army officers occupied the building. Some changes were made in the use of the rooms; for example, the kitchen of former assistant keeper George Warrington on the main floor became the galley and his living room the mess hall for the entire staff. The basement kitchen of head keeper Thomas Buckridge was converted into a recreation room. In addition, a backup water cistern built in 1912 was converted into a coal bin.[172]

Civilian keepers pose with members of the military at Montauk Point Lighthouse in 1942. Standing are head keeper Thomas Buckridge, second from left, Jack Miller to his immediate left, and George Warrington at far right. By mid 1943 the Army was in full control of the lighthouse as part of the Eastern Coastal Defense Shield. (Arthur Dunne Collection)

Part of the lighthouse operation included the construction of the Artillery Fire Control Tower, built in 1943 several feet east of the lighthouse tower. Within this solid 65-foot structure, artillery fire was coordinated with the 16-inch guns at Camp Hero. Originally covered in camouflage paint, the tower was used to survey the surrounding waters for the presence of enemy submarines.

Staff Sergeant Arthur Dunne (1916-2009) began his tour of service at the lighthouse in July 1942. In an interview in August 2008, Art explained that his assignment at Montauk was to install and operate a radar station. By the time the three civilian lighthouse keepers left the station in April 1943, construction of the radar tower was underway, as was the barracks overlooking Turtle Cove, southwest of the lighthouse. According to Art, the radar tower was built in separate sections each raised with a crane and placed one atop the other. The installation of steel rods strengthened the fortification. As noted in *Living on the Edge: Life at the Montauk Point Lighthouse 1930-1945*:

> *Inside the tower was contained highly sensitive equipment, including Seacoast Artillery microwave radar, known as SCXR-582, used for harbor patrol and detection of surface craft and low-flying planes. In addition, the radio navigation system known as LORAN (Long Range Aid to Navigation) was located here…The IFF system (Identification Friend or Foe) was used here and PQI enlarged one hundred feet of the baseline for the 16-inch guns in place at neighboring Camp Hero.*[173]

The wartime operation at the lighthouse was unknown to the public. Said Art, "Our unit was completely separate from the military at Camp Hero. As a matter of fact, there was no record of me even being out there at all! The radar operation was top secret."[174]

The operation and the radar station were considered so significant that the standing orders were to self-destruct in the event of an enemy land attack. At the prospect of self-destructing, Art mused, "I always wondered whether I'd do it."[175]

The radar tower at Montauk Lighthouse was designated a Harbor Entrance Observation Post and had direct communication with the Harbor Defense Command Post and the head Observation Post on Fisher's Island. A radar station for general surveillance was operated from the top of the tower.

The following paragraphs contain information about the Fire Control Tower from an article by Kurt Kahofer.

Harbor Defense Systems were established as part of the Eastern Coastal Defense Shield. The Harbor Defense of Long Island Sound (HDLIS) included the tip of Long Island, the Long Island Sound, and the coast from Southampton to Montauk. Each system controlled numerous harbors that constituted the approach to a major port, in this case, New York. The HDLIS was intended to protect industrial cities along the shores of southern Connecticut, part of the New Jersey coast, and the New York Metropolitan Area. Within the system was a Harbor Entrance Command Post, Fire Control Stations, gun batteries, and support structures. The Command Post for the HDLIS was on Mount Prospect, Fisher's Island.

Construction of the Fire Tower adjacent to the Montauk Point Lighthouse was photographed in 1942. The tower was built in separate sections, each raised with a crane and placed one atop the other. The addition of steel rods strengthened the fortification. (Arthur Dunne Collection)

The six-story Fire Control Station at the Montauk Point Lighthouse was equipped with two telescopes. One Azimuth telescope would take a reading on a target's location, while the other would aid in pinpointing where the guns in nearby batteries (in this case at Camp Hero) would be aimed. Stations worked in pairs to locate a single target, the point where their sight lines crossed providing the exact target location.

Built of splinter-proof concrete by the Army Corps of Engineers, the tower was designated as Location 16 Site 2C of the HDLIS. Location 16 refers to Camp Hero and Site 2C was one of numerous sites within

Location 16. Originally covered with camouflage paint, the tower appears totally white today.

The tower was intended to cover the following gun batteries:

- Battery No. 12 at Wilderness Point, Fishers Island. Guns were delivered to this site but never mounted.
- A site three miles east of Watch Hill, Rhode Island was planned but not built.
- Battery No. 3, Construction 216, Camp Hero. This was equipped with two 6-inch guns.

The Fire Control Station at Montauk Point was used as the Harbor Entrance Observation Post – 1, the most important surveillance station in the HDLIS.[176]

Once completed, the fire tower was covered with camouflage paint. The radar operation at Montauk Light was top secret. Note the fog signal to the right of the tower. The white building in the foreground is the old outhouse, in use by civilian keepers until plumbing was installed at the light station in 1938. This image shows the tower in 1943. (Arthur Dunne Collection)

## Camp Hero

Then there was the most famous Montauk military installation of all—Camp Hero. In early January 1942 the U. S. Government took title to 468 acres adjacent to the lighthouse at Montauk Point for "a battery site and for related military purposes." The order was signed by Secretary of War Henry Stimson (1867-1950).[177] Thus began the military history of Camp Hero.

Plans for the creation of the HDLIS were in progress as early as June 1940, but logistical problems

Overlooking Turtle Cove, the barracks at Montauk Point was constructed by the Army in 1942 and could house thirty men. The small white structure above the barracks was a sentry post, which is still extant. (Arthur Dunne Collection)

Once presenting a warm, friendly and inviting appearance, World War II changed the look of the Montauk Lighthouse property to one of "no trespassing" and "keep out." It appears here in 1943. (Arthur Dunne Collection)

at certain sites had to be resolved first. At Camp Hero, for example, it had to be decided whether to use the old Wyandanee Hotel on the Old Montauk Highway near the Point as a barracks.

The base was named for Major General Andrew Hero, Jr. (1868-1942), a man who rose though the ranks, first as a Second Lieutenant in 1891 to Major General in 1926. During the Spanish-American War he helped train the 3rd Division, III Army Corps and later taught at West Point. During WWI he was promoted to brigadier general and commanded the 154th Field Artillery Brigade (79th Division) and saw action in France. In 1926 he became Chief of Coast Artillery Corps, a position he held until his retirement in 1930. His father had been an officer in the Confederate Army during the Civil War and saw action at the Battle of Gettysburg.

During his tenure with the Coast Artillery Corps, in the summer of 1929, Hero participated in a simulated attack on New York City. His assignment was to defend the city and keep its harbor clear. Rear Admiral William Carey Cole (1868-1935), who played the role of the "enemy," led a "full-fledged battle fleet" from a base in Rhode Island, aiming to choke off a fleet of U. S. fighting ships in New York Harbor. Stationed at Fort Hancock at Sandy Hook, New Jersey, General Hero prepared for battle, which lasted three days. The invaders claimed to have disabled Fort Hancock by destroying its observation and control towers and then coming close enough to "pound the fort to powder." General Hero, however, claimed his defenses were successful, citing the destruction of "two battleships, one cruiser, five destroyers, many a seaplane, and the repulse of a night landing party." The battle between the Admiral and the General also resulted in the "destruction" of lower Manhattan, East River bridges, the Brooklyn Navy Yard and huge ammunition dumps at Jersey City.[178]

The site for Camp Hero reportedly had a military history that went back to the days of the American Revolution when both American and British ships conducted firing practice with cannons against the bluffs near Montauk Point. They supposedly conducted similar practices during the War of 1812.

In order to construct Camp Hero, the former estate of New York Representative Lathrop Brown

A rare view of Old Montauk Highway, with Montauk Lighthouse on the bluff in the distance, was captured in 1922. This section of the road, once an adventurous ride to the Point because of the hills, was eliminated with the construction of Camp Hero in 1942. (Courtesy of the Queens Borough Public Library, Long Island Division, Eugene L. Armbruster Photographs)

Shown is the Lathrop Brown estate and windmill, ca.1940. This bucolic scene abruptly changed two years later when the estate was broken up and the mill was moved to Wainscott, Long Island for the construction of Camp Hero. (Courtesy of Suffolk County Historical Society)

was broken up, including the removal of a historic windmill built in Southampton in 1813. It was moved to Wainscott, Long Island in 1852 and then to Brown's estate in 1922. It stood on a cliff overlooking Turtle Cove just west of the lighthouse. Brown converted the ground floor into a sitting room, and turned the upper two small rooms into guest bedrooms. Along with the Brown estate, neighboring properties were sold to the Government to make way for the military base. People were told they had six months to remove structures on their land or they would be torn down. The sturdy old mill withstood many a storm, including the great hurricane of September 21, 1938 that damaged only the door and some window glass. Even the arms of the mill survived intact.[179] It stands today in the Georgica Association at Wainscott, Long Island. The main house was divided and moved to various locations in Montauk.

In 1999, Carl Dordelman of East Hampton recalled the days when Camp Hero was under construction:

> *I worked down at Camp Hero, when they were buildin' that...I was only fourteen, fifteen years old. Yeah, they had kids working down there. We were planting all that camouflage shrubbery and everything...They had to recruit child labor because there wasn't anybody else left around, you know, it was wartime. And I went down there and planted shrubbery for the camouflage. I remember it very well...They picked us up in East Hampton by the busload and took us down there every day.*[180]

Montauk native and current resident, Frank Tuma (born 1924) lived above the current Shagwong Tavern in town in his early years. His father, Frank Tuma, Sr., was a member of the Coast Guard and was stationed at Ditch Plain as early as 1913. In a March 2010 interview with the author, Frank Jr. recalled working at Camp Hero in the summer during his college days: "I worked on the construction of the steel lathes in the batteries that housed the 16-inch guns, for a big 81 cents an hour."[181]

According to a report by the Army, establishing the base had its problems, in particular the guns:

> The movement of the guns was a huge problem for the Army…The guns were originally transported across the rickety Shinnecock Bridge, and later by railroad. The railroad proved to be a slow and unwieldy method, as well as costly, so the Army worked out an arrangement to transport the guns by barge. This also proved to be a slow, dangerous and costly process and was soon given up. The Army finally built its own bridge and the last of the big guns…thundered across a specially constructed pontoon bridge.[182]

*East Hampton Star* editor and writer Everett Rattray described the procession of Colonial Sand and Gravel trucks heading for Camp Hero:

> They came heavily laden from some quarry far to the west, thundering past every two or three minutes. Through East Hampton and Amagansett they roared, the pounding of their wheels cracking chimneys and gradually crumbling the yellowish concrete with which Route 27 was surfaced in those days. Across Napeague Beach they trundled, bearing sand like coals to Newcastle over a landscape all sand to another landscape equally sandy, sand to be made into concrete and poured into hallows dug in the sand of Montauk Point, concrete for great-gun emplacements.[183]

The entire facility, including Army, Navy and Coast Guard constituents, was officially known as the "U.S. Military Reservation," but it was known locally as "Camp Hero." The base, which grew to 278 acres in size, was also used as a training facility and target range, with guns being fired at offshore targets. To protect it from enemy attack the base was disguised as a New England fishing village. Concrete bunkers had windows painted on them and ornamental roofs with fake dormers. The gymnasium was made to resemble a church complete with steeple. At its height during the war, the facility had 600 enlisted men and 37 officers stationed there.

Frank (Shank) Dickinson reported in a March 2010 interview that around 1943-44 Army personnel were camped in tents in Deep Hollow, where horses and cattle graze today on the south side of Montauk Highway opposite Third House. Dickinson's family has owned and operated the Deep Hollow Ranch for many generations.[184]

The public knew there were guns at Camp Hero but were unaware of the size of the camp, the number of personnel, or the purpose of the operation. But hearing the periodic firing of the mighty guns in exercises showed Americans "and anyone else concerned that Camp Hero protected the southeastern tip of Long Island, well out into the Atlantic Ocean and with other forts protected all waterways leading to New York City, Providence and New Haven."[185]

The 16-inch Navy guns were originally built for a class of battleships that was never constructed, due to the Washington Naval Treaty signed by the United States, Great Britain, Japan, France, and Italy in 1922 and designed to prevent a naval arms race that had begun after World War I. Originally out in the open, the newly built batteries were casemated and camouflaged with netting and foliage during the 1930s to protect them from aerial attacks.

Montauk native and current resident Dave Webb (born 1937), who is a member of the Lighthouse Committee of the Montauk Historical Society, recalled in March 2010 the arrival of the big guns, the construction of the batteries that housed them, and how the townspeople prepared when the guns were to be test-fired:

> My father was a batch concrete inspector. He told me that there was so much steel in the concrete canopies over the guns they had to reduce the size of the stones in the concrete between the steel. I recall the 16-inchers [guns] going up the highway [to Camp Hero] at a very slow pace. I remember being informed, I guess by telephone, that they were going to test the guns, so we had to open our windows so the shock waves wouldn't break the glass.[186]

The guns at Camp Hero were powerful and capable of firing a 2,000-pound shell a distance of thirty miles with accuracy. When testing was conducted as part of wartime drills, windows rattled miles away, unsettling many residents in Montauk village six miles distant. Montauk resident Clancy Pitts recalled liquor bottles falling off shelves in the Shagwong Inn when the guns roared.[187] Once in place at the site, the guns were manned by troops from the 11th Coast Artillery Regiment and the 242nd Connecticut National Guard Coast Artillery Regiment.

Milton Miller, who was born in 1915, joined the Coast Guard when he joined the service in 1938. He remains a vibrant outspoken citizen of East Hampton. In an August 2010 interview, he shared his thoughts about the defenses at Camp Hero:

> The only defense there was the radar. One of the best things they had down there. The rest of it didn't amount to a damn. Because, what are you gonna do if you have a regular invasion? Ya had the 16-inch guns, what are you gonna hit with a 16-inch gun? You could move 'em up and down, back and forth. In the Civil War days when ships was under sail, you might hit something.

> You needed three cross bearings before they could fire them guns. Someone had to take a bearing at the lighthouse. Gardiner's Island had one. There was another location along Napeague Beach but I forget where it was at. Then they gotta get this all coordinated together, gotta elevate that gun; I mean, where did they think a destroyer going 40-50 miles would be by the time they got their bearings?[188]

According to former chairman of the Lighthouse Committee of the Montauk Historical Society, Dick White, when the big guns came to town his father took pictures of them as they rolled down the main street by the family's drug store. "But I guess someone ratted on him, and somebody came to look at the camera. Well, in the drug store, my father sold cameras. So he took the film out and put the cameras on the shelf, put prices on them. So when the guy came in and asked if he had a camera, my dad said, 'I have several. Which one would you like to buy?' They never did see those pictures."[189]

One of the huge 16-inch guns at Camp Hero is pictured ca.1943. There were four of this type of weapon (plus two 6-inch guns) in position at Camp Hero during WWII. Any one of the 16-inch guns could fire a 2000-pound shell a distance of 30- miles with pin-point accuracy. (Montauk Point Lighthouse Museum)

Three self-sufficient batteries (numbered 112, 113, and 216) were constructed. Battery 216 had two M1903A2 6-inch guns delivered in January of 1943. Construction began on Battery 113 on March 23, 1942 and was completed on June 5th. It was renamed Battery Dunn on August 10th in honor of Colonel John M. Dunn, who was Director of Military Intelligence for a time during World War I. Battery 113 had two Navy MKIIM1 16-inch casemated guns that were installed by June 5, 1943. Battery 112 guns were identical to those in 113 and were completed by January 12, 1944. In addition, 37mm weapons and .50-caliber anti-aircraft weapon platoons protected the camp from air attacks.

Batteries 112 and 113 used 16-inch, 2,240-pound projectiles, while Battery 216 handled 6-inch, 90-pound high explosive rounds and 6-inch, 105-pound armor piercing rounds. Munitions for the guns were stored at an undisclosed location off-site.

A series of tunnels connected the huge concrete batteries. There also were anti-aircraft and machine gun emplacements. Scattered about were numerous spotting towers that were manned around the clock.

The Eastern Coastal Defense Shield extended from Maine to the Florida Keys. In the Northeast it consisted of eight fortifications designed to protect cities between New York and Providence, Rhode Island. These included Fort Mansfield at Watch Hill, Rhode Island; Fort Trumbull at New London, Connecticut; Fort Michie on Great Gull Island, New York; Fort H. G. Wright on Fisher's Island, New York (the headquarters for the group); Fort Terry on Plum Island, New York; Fort Tyler on Gardiner's Point, New York; and Camp Hero at Montauk Point, considered "the most mysterious, the most recently active post and the most heavily camouflaged."[190]

The function of fire control stations was to track incoming targets. The following paragraph describes the procedure:

> *Typically, a team of six men would report observations to one gun battery. Some of the men were "observers" tracking the target, while others were "spotters" watching the trajectory of fired rounds. Observations at each fire control station were made with two telescopes, and fire control stations usually worked in pairs using geometry to pinpoint a target. Visual observation was supplemented by radar.[191]*

Going west from Camp Hero to Quogue, Long Island, a distance of about 40 miles, at intervals of three to four miles "two and a half story tall, fake private homes" were constructed. Armed with troops and weapons, they were part of the defense network protecting Long Island's shores. The inland-facing half of the buildings was simple wood clapboard that gave the appearance of a beachfront home. On the ocean side "the forms into which the concrete was poured were made with overlapping wood boards to make the hardened concrete look like wooden clapboard."

The Army chose vacant lands for the homes, told the owners what they planned to do, and after the war the structures were left to the landowners. With walls of concrete four feet thick, they were converted into private homes and still stand today.[192]

Some twenty-seven of these stations were constructed to serve the HDLIS. Those on the East End of Long Island included the following extant stations, as noted by Adele Cramer in her report, "Ditch Plains Artillery Fire Control Stations":

- Gardiner's Island. Located on Whale Hill, it combined the cottage and tower type of station and resembled a windmill.
- Camp Hero. Designed in the cottage style, it was used as the battery commander's station for the commanders of batteries 112 and 113 at Camp Hero.
- Shagwong Point. Known locally as the Lindley House within Theodore Roosevelt County Park, it was built in the cottage style.
- Hither Hills. Two stations remain along the Old Montauk Highway. The first, at 251 Old Montauk Highway, and the second, known as the Warren House, stands next door.
- Amagansett. Situated at the foot of Whaler's Lane and currently known as the Ocean House.

Seen here in 1985 is one of the "cottages" used as the battery commander's station for the commanders of Batteries 112 and 113 at Camp Hero during World War II. (Marge Winski photo)

The commander's building at the Ditch Plains site (now Shadmoor State Park) is no longer extant, but two fire control structures survive, though in such poor condition that they have lost much of their original character. The site, designed location 13 within the HDLIS, was the second largest installation after Camp Hero. The land, formerly the estate of Alfred M. Hoyt, was purchased by the government early in 1943. The property was ideally suited for military use because of natural hills that provided the necessary height for the telescopes. Construction of all buildings was completed early in 1944.

The fire control station building at Ditch Plains, pictured in October 1997, was the second largest installation after Camp Hero within the Harbor Defense of Long Island Sound. It is now part of Shadmoor State Park, Montauk. (Montauk Point Lighthouse Museum)

During the waning days of the war at least twenty-four men were stationed at the Ditch Plains site. In addition to the two fire control stations there was a radar tower, two generator shelter units, and a "Type D" building which contained living quarters, a mess hall, kitchen, and store room. It appeared as a wood-framed one-story large ranch-style home, with two covered entry porches and false chimneys.[193] This building no longer exists.

According to Dan Rattiner in *Dan's Papers*, The Westhampton Air Base (now the Francis S. Gabreski Airport) served as the base where all alerts were radioed: "An enemy could be sighted, and the planes at Westhampton—bombers, fighters and helicopters—could be scrambled and sent out to deal with the situation." The Army and Air Force maintained stations here until about 1960.[194]

After the war the huge concrete batteries at Camp Hero were used as fallout shelters, "stocked with dry biscuits and canned water against Armageddon."[195]

Margaret Erskine Cahill, who lived at Montauk decades ago, recalled the war years at Montauk: "The blackout at Montauk during the war was stringent. No one was allowed on the beach after sundown. We had no neighbors then, within screaming distance; no telephone, radio, or electricity...Due to gas and tire-rationing, we had no car."[196]

Against the wishes of her parents, and with her husband in the Navy, Cahill took her young children to Montauk in the summer of 1942, armed only with an old machete and a ball peen hammer for protection. When her mother asked, "But what would you do down there, in the event of a bombing or invasion," Cahill said she learned how to say "Welcome" in German, just in case![197]

Vinnie Grimes shared these thoughts about Camp Hero and the Montauk of World War II:

> *You had the Coast Guard up at the lighthouse, the Navy at Fort Pond, the Army at Camp Hero, the Signal Corps was out at the lighthouse at that time. The Signal Corps put a*

*lower amp bulb in there. They had a lot of ship movement out here. The Coast Guard Auxiliary would take off from Montauk and Connecticut. These were yachts that would patrol the coast, so you had to have a light because those boats didn't have radar yet.*

*When they brought the 16-inch gun barrels out here to Camp Hero and they had Colonial Sand and Gravel hauling concrete in here by the truckloads, we didn't know what was going on. But I could sit on the bluffs in front of my house at Sand Piper Hill and see the flashes out in the ocean- it was German U-boats hitting tankers and cargo ships that were headed for Europe to help in the war effort. We were closer to harm than we realized.*

*When World War II came about, Franklin Delano Roosevelt got on the radio and gave those Fireside Chats of his, saying "We're not gonna stand for this" and "We will win". Well, everybody wanted to do something. I was too young to get in the service by about 2 years, and I was the oldest in a close knit family. If I'd a-gone in and lied about my age my father would have followed me and killed me. It was that way. The oldest one in the family was in charge of everybody. If any of my brothers or my sister did anything wrong it was my fault; I shoulda been there to correct them.*

*During the war I worked where Herb's Market is in town. We lived up at Sand Piper Hill and me and my brother would walk home every night. Well, you weren't supposed to do that. Better to go all the way to Ditch Plains, take the road and come that way. We would go in where Shadmoor [State Park] is, and when we hit the cliffs we'd run like a son-of-a-gun because they were patrolling there all the time. Why we never got shot I don't know! How many times the guy would holler "halt!" and we'd run! They got even with us; they shot my dog one night. They hollered "halt!" and he didn't halt. Did they think he was a German or what?*

*The Coast Guard would patrol the beach and the Signal Corps would patrol the bluffs. Sometimes when the Coast Guard was down there and wanted to relieve himself the damned Army guy would shoot at his feet. They finally ended that because they had to show how many cartridges they had. If any were used up they had to explain, give a good reason. They shot cows up in Bridgehampton. You holler "halt" to a cow in a field and you know damn well it's not a human!*[198]

Montauk citizens also were involved in the war effort as airplane spotters. Before America's involvement in the war, simulated drills were run. The following spotters—Clifford (CW) and Nellie Windsor (NW) and Charles Tuma (CT)—were interviewed by Tony Martin (TM) on Major Bowes Chrysler Hour radio program in 1940. They spoke proudly of their service to their country:

*TM: How did you happen to go in for this civilian volunteer observation work?*
*CW: Well…it's an American Legion activity here, and I've been post commander six years. It seemed to me that this was one of my duties.*
*TM: I see. And so you appoint your own observers…I understand your wife is one of them.*

*CW: Yes; she was one of the first volunteers.*

*TM: How do you do, Mrs. Windsor. Are you on duty today?*

*NW: No, I was on the morning watch from six to eight…We're up early out here. We have so much to do…Somebody has to do it- and we're interested in what's going on. I don't think I'd feel very good if I weren't doing it…*

*TM: Now, this is Charles Tuma, who owns and operates the fishing-boat Dawn. How's fishing, Captain?*

*CT: Fishing's not bad; but fishing for airplanes is a little tougher.*

*TM: Were you on duty today?*

*CT: No, I go on at four…Cliff schedules me when he knows I'm here.*

*TM: Think these fishing boats that operate off here might be useful, Captain, for spotting airplanes?*

*CT: Well, the ones that have ship-to-shore radio will…In case of war, though, I imagine we'd be more valuable looking for submarines. We all know these shores pretty well, you know…*

*TM: And here, ladies and gentlemen, is a cross-section of the kind of Americans who are performing this very important and very specialized task of spotting and reporting the "enemy" bombers as they approach our shores. Theirs is a very real part of the defense of our nation…The Army depends upon these civilian volunteers- without them, there would be no staving off an aerial invasion of our shores…From morning to night, they watch the skies- and it is their reports upon which the Air Force's tactics are based. They are the most important citizens of America today.[199]*

According to a U. S. Army report in December 1996, there was limited chemical warfare training at Camp Hero in 1945 but the exact location is unknown. The report states:

*Records indicate that on 22 February 1945, Battery "A" Coast Artillery Battalion (Mustard – HD) held a Gas Identification Detonation Exercise. During this exercise, men were sent into clouds of mustard, Phosgene, and lewisite. On this day the weather conditions were less favorable (inversion) and the clouds hung close to the ground; thus, a high number of men experienced irritations on their faces and arms. Because the inversion conditions were the cause of the men's irritations, it was stated that the exercises would only be held on favorable days.*

*The report concluded, 'it was believed that this was a singular or infrequent training event at Camp Hero conducted by a specialized, external training source'.[200]*

Hidden among numerous documents, clippings, photos, and other artifacts in the attic of the Montauk Point Lighthouse Museum is a typed page entitled "Proud Visitor" (author unknown). It describes the final chapter in the history of a former Nazi military vessel as it came to New York about a year and half after the surrender of Germany. The passing vessel must have been quite a sight for Coast Guard personnel at the Montauk Point Lighthouse, a final sign of a long and destructive war:

In this March 12, 1945 image of Montauk Point Lighthouse, near the end of the war in Europe, the ominous fire tower looms over the bluff. Note the bunker built into the top of the bluff itself. With neighboring Camp Hero's guns at the ready and the radar operations at the lighthouse, Montauk typified the image of Gibraltar itself. (Montauk Point Lighthouse Museum)

*In order to reach New London on August 12, 1946, the "Eagle" had to pass under the gaze of the Montauk Lighthouse for the first time. It was also the first time under way with an all American crew.*

*The day before, her compliment of German officers and sailors had been taken off by military police as the ship lay at anchor in the Hudson River near the George Washington Bridge.*

*It was a bitter disappointment to the younger Germans who had known the 300-foot barque as "Horst Wessel." They'd helped put her back together after the war. They were the experienced hands during the trip across the Atlantic. Their captain, Berthold Schnibbe, with the help of a brave German foremast hand, had probably saved the renamed "Eagle" from foundering in a hurricane only days before. The Germans had friends among the U. S. Coast Guard crew; Americans they'd shown the ropes and who, in return, had promised to show them the states.*

*But the most terrible war had ended only months before. Unspeakable crimes had been committed. And lies; the Americans were amazed when the Germans remarked at how quickly New York City had been rebuilt as the ship passed en route to their anchorage. Then everyone was silent as "Eagle" slid by the Statue of Liberty, her sails in tatters from the hurricane, from the entire crew's near-death experience.*

*The M. P. s came and took them away.*

The military presence on Montauk during World War II had a lasting impact on the small, previously quiet and remote community. Over five hundred acres of land, both private and State owned, was acquired for military purposes, forcing local residents to evacuate their homes within a short period of time. The Old Montauk Highway became a dead end road two miles short of Montauk Point, the last two miles of the highway being absorbed within the Camp Hero grounds. The former fishing village at Fort Pond Bay ceased to exist, basically replaced by Army and Navy facilities, with some homes relocated and most demolished. Security was so tight during wartime that anyone in the area was subject to questioning. There was an influx of new residents at the end of the war, since some of the men stationed on Montauk remained and married local women.

The Navy had relocated the fishing village at Fort Pond Bay to create the torpedo testing station. They occupied Montauk Manor and the Fisher Office Tower. A Coast Guard patrol base was established on Star Island in Lake Montauk. The Army had occupied the Montauk Point Lighthouse and established a radar station there. Camp Hero was established with an Army base constructed to resemble a fishing village from the air, armed with some of the heaviest and most potent weapons of the day. Military personnel and local civilians were on alert and patrol. More than at any other time in its history, Montauk had indeed become a military town—an American Gibraltar.

# CHAPTER 9

# The Cold War Years and Camp Hero 1946 – 1980s

AT THE CONCLUSION of World War II Camp Hero was temporarily shut down and used as a training facility by the Army Reserves. On February 7, 1947 Battery 113 was placed on inactive status. On July 31st the entire camp was placed on inactive status. By February 1949 the great guns were being dismantled, with nickel and steel going to Buffalo, New York, scrap to the Bethlehem plant at Philadelphia, and brass and non-ferrous metals going to other facilities in Philadelphia. Some structures were torn down. The town of Montauk, once a lively center of military activity, "had been returned to the surf casters and the sea gulls."[201] The great 16-inch guns also were removed from installations at Fort Wright on Fishers Island and at Great Gull Island. When Camp Hero was utilized by the Air Force in later years, Jim Sullivan of Montauk was stationed there (1957-1958) and noted that the huge bunkers that housed the guns were put to use as storage facilities, and "during practice drills in the event of a nuclear attack we used them as shelters."[202]

The camp property was declared surplus by the Army on December 31, 1949.

In 1946, Fred Houseknecht was stationed with the Army at Camp Hero and remained there until he was discharged from the service in 1949. Born in 1926 near Williamsport, Pennsylvania, he was so affected by the beautiful scenery from the cliffs of Montauk that he did not want to leave. "If they said I could have stayed there I would have signed on for another three years," he said in 2004.[203] He was trained to provide diesel-powered electricity to operate the huge guns.

In an interview at the East Deck Motel on Montauk in September 2009, Fred spoke of his years as a sergeant at Camp Hero:

> It was 1946 when I first went there, and it was on a caretaker basis. Our main fort was at Fort H. G. Wright on Fisher's Island. That was our headquarters. We had Fort Terry which was on Plum Island, and Fort Michie which was on Little Gull Island, so we were pretty well surrounded. We had 16-inch guns out here in two batteries, and a battery of 6-inch. We had a 6-inch battery on Plum Island, and a 3-inch on Little Gull.
>
> We maintained the guns at Montauk after the war ended. While I was there we started cuttin' 'em up and takin' em out. We burnt all the powder from them right there on the base and down on the beach. It didn't pay to have it hauled anyplace else 'cause it was too hard to keep. If it got any moisture in it, it was gone. The shells we had weighed 2200 pounds. They could fire 38 miles with point accuracy.

*We had to keep the fire lanes clear. We had to keep them all cut all around the perimeter. That was one of the biggest things we had to do. Sometimes I'd have a work detail of 35-40 men under my command. One time we had a big fire up there. For years we had dumped the cuttings over the cliff and somehow they caught fire. The fire department was up there and we had one big time!*

*We also had to meet the boats down at the Navy dock in Montauk and bring supplies over. We also took care of seven big wells that pumped water for the base.*[204]

Fred Houseknecht was stationed at Camp Hero 1946-1949 and was responsible for maintaining the big guns and keeping the fire lanes clear. He appears here in 1947. (Courtesy of Fred Houseknecht)

Fred Houseknecht, with a loyal friend, perches atop one of the huge 16-inch guns at Camp Hero. The guns were dismantled in 1949. (Courtesy of Fred Houseknecht)

Fred Houseknecht, pictured in September 2009, remains very active in Montauk. Fred is proud of his military service at Camp Hero. (Author photo)

In 1952, three years after his discharge from Camp Hero, Fred Houseknecht opened a construction business and built numerous homes and motels on Montauk, including the Maisonettes (now the Ocean End Motel), which was the first motel in town. Others would follow—the Montauk Motel, Snug Harbor Motel, Fort Pond Lodge, and the Oceanside Beach Resort.

However, Fred is proudest of the East Deck Motel at Ditch Plain, Montauk, which was previously owned by his father-in-law, Sam Cox. In 1955 they purchased Olsen's Cottages at Navy Road on Fort Pond Bay, an assemblage of 20 small cottages which they moved to the Ditch Plain site. They were spaced sixteen feet apart, and were subsequently connected by motel units built in between by Fred in the late 1960s. The motel is still operated by the family.

Fred is still active in construction work around Montauk, but when it comes to real heavy work he looks to his helpers. Says Fred: "Now I just point."

Montauk native Dave Webb remembers going to the railroad station where the cut up guns from Camp Hero were taken: "I remember taking little chunks of them home, thinking I could sell the steel. I would put a chunk in the basket of my bicycle."[205]

Early in 1948 the U. S. Department of Agriculture planned to establish a laboratory to study hoof and mouth disease in cattle and considered Camp Hero as the site for the operation. As a result of opposition from the Suffolk Board of Supervisors, the proposed plan never materialized on Montauk. An Animal Disease Center was ultimately established off Long Island's North Fork on Plum Island in 1954 and continues to function.

In response to the growing threat of the Soviet Union's nuclear capability and their deployment of long range strategic bomber aircraft, in June of 1948 the Air Force deployed its first radar set at Camp Hero, making it one of three early warning radar sites in the northeast.* The data was transmitted to the 26th Air Division's Air Defense Control Center in Roslyn, Long Island. Over the next few years, various other radar systems would be in place at Camp Hero.

During the Korean War, which began on June 25, 1950, restrictions were imposed on Montauk mariners, as they had been during World War II. A fan-shaped area 15-miles out to sea was banned from use by vessels so the Army could conduct anti-aircraft weapon practice at Camp Hero. However, boats were permitted to sail past the firing point close to the bluffs.[206]

In the 1950s a major concern for the U. S. was Soviet long-range bombers with nuclear weapons. As part of the defense of our shores, in November 1950 the Army transferred the western portion of Camp Hero to the 773rd Aircraft Control and Warning (AC&W) Squadron. At this time the base was run jointly by the Army and the Air Force, with the Army in the eastern portion and the Air Force in the western portion.

The AC&W was part of the Eastern Air Defense Force until February 6, 1952 when it became part of the 26th Air Division. It provided surveillance for detection, identification, and interception of aircraft entering its area of responsibility and was a vital link in the nation's aerospace defense network.

On January 24, 1951 Camp Hero was withdrawn from surplus by the Army and designated for use as a firing range and field exercise area for antiaircraft artillery (AAA) from Fort Totten, New York.

In February 1951 the First Army moved personnel and equipment from Fort Totten in Bayside, Queens to conduct maneuvers at Camp Hero. The huge amount of relocated equipment included anti-aircraft batteries that came via flatcars aboard the Long Island Railroad, and "a motor caravan made up of some 40 trucks, 20 jeeps and four or five busses crammed with men thundered through South Side villages [en route to Montauk]."[207]

The journey had a significant obstacle. The 90-mm guns and their carriers, weighing over 60 tons apiece, had to stop at Canoe Place, Hampton Bays. The old steel railroad bridge over the Shinnecock Canal only had a 12-ton capacity. The Army found a way around the problem:

> *While the guns rode safely over the newer and stronger railroad bridge a few hundred yards distant, the 69th AA Gun Battalion convoy made a slow and cautious passage over the elderly highway span. Truck and trailer units were temporarily unhooked and the trailers were towed across by cable. It was reported that the old bridge creaked and groaned but held up.*[208]

Dick White recalled those days when the soldiers came to Montauk:

> *The batteries would come out to Montauk at night, and there would be a whole line of vehicles, starting with the jeep that included the unit commander, followed by the trucks with the soldiers inside, followed by the cannons, followed by the halftracks, followed by the cook shed, followed by the tool shed, etc. Everything was on wheels; these were self contained units. They came right through town and set up camp.*

> *They would be there for a while and fire at drones carrying targets. Initially there was aircraft towing these targets, but they found it more and more difficult trying to find guys to fly the plane, because an errant shot would take them out!*

> *I was in the 7th grade at the time, and the classroom I was in faced the ocean. All of a sudden you would see black flak marks in the sky where the shells had exploded. And*

*maybe a minute or so later you would hear the report- boom-boom, boom, boom. Boom-boom, boom, boom.*

*The crews would be there for about two weeks and train. Then one night the whole parade went the other way. Everything was packed up, and here comes the jeep, then the truck with the men, the cannons, and so on. And about a week later, here comes another group and they would set up camp and practice for two weeks.* [209]

The Army occupation caused alarm over the effect it would have on the fishing industry at Montauk. The following article appeared in *The Long Islander* on March 8, 1951:

*A First Army order establishing a restricted area in the Atlantic Ocean off Montauk will virtually ruin the resort and fishing industries of the picturesque land's-end community, it was charged at a meeting of the Montauk Businessmen's Association Tuesday night. Plans were mapped out for a petition-signing and letter-writing campaign to induce the Department of the Army to cancel or modify the edict banning all marine traffic from an area extending from the west shore of Block Island to Amagansett between the hours of 7:30 a.m. and 4:30 p.m. each weekday, April 3 to Dec. 31. The purpose of the order is to clear the area for anti-aircraft gunnery practice from Fort Hero which was reactivated three weeks ago.* [210]

Though both commercial and pleasure fishermen voiced complaints about the restrictions, they won the concession of the safe area close to shore so that they could return to their docks even if they had to go out of their way. [213]

Periodically, articles appeared in local newspapers indicating when practices were to be conducted and what procedures were to be followed. The following is an example which appeared in the *East Hampton Star* on January 31, 1952:

*Notice is hereby given that First Army will conduct Antiaircraft Artillery practice fire in Atlantic Ocean off Montauk Point, New York, during the period of 4 to 29 February daily, except Saturdays, Sundays or legal holidays, between the hours of 9:00 a.m. and 4 p.m., local time.*

*Such firings as are conducted prior to 9:00 a. m....will be occasional individual rounds fired at fixed points for testing purposes...and will involve no restrictions on navigation.*

*During the regular periods of firing, a large red flag will be displayed from the observation tower on the reservation and the area will be patrolled by Army vessels and aircraft. No vessel shall enter or remain in the danger area during the times of firing, except that navigation will be permitted through a portion of the area extending about one mile offshore around Montauk Point.* [212]

When the Air Force took over in 1951 and renamed the area the Montauk Air Force Station, its primary function was to be part of a nationwide early warning radar system. For nearly 30 years the Air Force used sophisticated radar and tracking equipment that was set up on site. Various types of radar units were installed during the 1950s with the designation "AN/FPS" (meaning Army-Navy Fixed, Radar, Search). At Camp Hero, AN/FPS-3 and AN/FPS-5 units were installed in 1952 and AN/FPS-8 medium range radar in 1955. In 1957, AN/FPS-20 radar was installed. Each of these systems had a range of more than 200 miles.

Munitions used included 90mm and 120mm guns, .50 caliber machine guns, and 3.5-inch rockets. An Air Defense Direction Center was established which provided radar surveillance for the detection, identification, and interception of all aircraft entering its territory.

Historically, a radar system was known to exist atop Prospect Hill on Montauk in 1942. In 1948, radar again operated there, most likely a LASH-Up radar site, "L-10." The original and LASH-Up sites sat where (or near) the more modern GATR (Ground to Air Transmit and Receive) site stands today, though inactive.

The LASH-Up system of radars was designed by the Air Force to cover the country's coastal centers and major nuclear production facilities. By 1949 there were seven such sites in the nation, and by 1951 there were fifty.

The GATR sites permitted controllers on the ground at the Air Force Station to communicate via UHF (and later VHF) radio with aircraft. As part of the SAGE (Semi-Automatic Ground Environment) project, GATR sites were updated with high-power tactical digital data links so that ground controllers could actually guide the interceptor aircraft to their targets. SAGE was an automated control system used by NORAD (North American Aerospace Defense Command) for tracking and intercepting enemy aircraft from the late 1950s to the 1980s.

The towers that now stand at the old Air Force Station on Montauk are no more than wooden telephone poles supporting types of VHF/UHF antennas.

Don Bender, a historical consultant, explained the importance of the Air Force Station in 1999: "[It] was sited at the extreme easterly end of Long Island so that its radar coverage would extend as far as possible in a seaward direction. It was the parent facility for the offshore radar platform known as Texas Tower Number Two. These fixed offshore radar platforms…transmitted directly to the Montauk Air Force Station."[213]

Originally there were plans to construct five Texas Towers in the northeast region. Resembling offshore oil rigs, their purpose was to extend existing coastal radar seaward. However, due to treacherous storms and waves, working at a Texas Tower site was a dangerous assignment and consequently the existence of the towers was short-lived. Tower #2 was located about 120 miles east of Chatham, Cape Cod and went into operation late in 1955. Personnel aboard the station were from Otis Air Force Base, Falmouth, MA. Shortly after Tower #4, located about 70 miles off the New York and New Jersey coasts, was destroyed in a storm in January 1961 with the loss of all aboard, Tower #2 was decommissioned. Tower #3, off Boston, was also shut down. Towers #1 and #5 were never built.

It wasn't all fun and games having the military on the East End in those days, as recalled by Carl Dordelman of East Hampton in 1999, referring to those "damn G.I.s":

*The bars made a fortune in those days…They were three, four deep at the bar, you know? These service guys. They'd all get tanked up…I remember one time one of them broke into Kelly's liquor store [in East Hampton]. Punched the whole front window out. Went in there and took bottles of booze. It wasn't really hard to find the guy, because I just followed the bottles. Main Street, all the way past the movie theater and in back of the VFW, he's laying in the parking lot out there, passed right out cold, the guy is.*[214]

Winford (Bill) Gronley of Mt. Clemens, MI (born 1930) was stationed at Camp Hero from March to November 1952 as a radio operator, keeping in communication with Navy picket ships that patrolled the ocean. He remembers his time there as being quiet but enjoyable, but he also remembered good times when the men went to East Hampton. When it was mentioned to him that sometimes the men tended to be a bit rowdy when they went to East Hampton he said, "Oh yeah, that happened," and laughed.

Gronley recalled that on one occasion he and two other men from the base decided to have dinner at the Montauk Manor. When they arrived there (in uniform) they were not permitted to enter because, according to Gronley, "there was a black tie affair going on. I never forgot that!"[215]

By 1957, the Army had switched from gun batteries to the new Nike guided missiles, which were mostly launched from desert areas of New Mexico. For that reason, and because by this time Soviet bombers could fly well above ground-based artillery, the Army closed the Camp Hero portion of the reservation in November 1957. The Air Force continued radar surveillance in the western section. The eastern section was donated to the State of New York, but being so close to the high security Air Force facility, it remained undeveloped.

First Lieutenant James (Jim) T. Sullivan (born 1930) was stationed at Camp Hero during 1957-1958. He "came as a bachelor, but left a married man after marrying a local girl, Barbara Gilmartin." He had already been in the Air Force for about five years, assigned to a number of fighter squadrons on the east and west coasts and in Newfoundland, and was recently transferred from Newcastle, Delaware to Montauk. According to Sullivan, the mission of the 773rd was to "direct, identify, intercept, and destroy if necessary, unknown or unfriendly aircraft and recover the fighters."[216]

While he was assigned to Camp Hero, about 200-250 men and about twenty officers were stationed there. His job at Camp Hero was duty controller and officer in charge of the NCO (non-commissioned officer) club.

Sullivan explained the operation of identifying a target at Camp Hero in an interview for the Montauk Library in March 2003:

*Usually you had a flight of two planes that went up. One went in to identify the target and the other would maintain a separation in case it was an unfriendly target. He would be in position to attack the target. Of course, you always had rules of engagement. You never engaged anything without proper approval. But the main thing was to get an ID.*

*Right off the coast of Montauk were Russian trawlers who were not doing much fishing (they were loaded with antennas), but were fishing to find out what type of communications we were using and what type of radar we had... Planes from Suffolk County Air Force Base (now Gabreski Airport) at Westhampton Beach would fly out to Montauk and buzz them to let them know we knew what they were doing.*[217]

Ken Jacob, who came to the base in 1964, recalled the activity surrounding the presence of Russian aircraft:

*They would take off from Cuba and as they would come up the coast we would be tracking them on the scope. You'd see the fighters coming from Suffolk in Westhampton and Otis Air Force Base [in Massachusetts] and you'd see the Russian bombers go out to sea out of our airspace. It was more or less routine; they tried to test the radar.*[218]

Jim Sullivan noted that Camp Hero was a great place to have a good time when one was off duty. He related two incidents that occurred while he was responsible for the NCO club:

*The club complained that they didn't have any music. The chaplain came out from Westhampton Beach and we discussed a church organ he no longer needed. We convinced him we could use it for church services at the base. That went very well until one Friday night he came out for an unexpected visit and there they were dancing to the organ at the NCO club and having a terrific party! But he still let us keep the organ.*

*We were friendly with the Lion's Club which held their meetings at the NCO club. One time, since I was club officer, we held a steak dinner for them. I had one of the cooks do the cooking. He set up a grill out the window and he was cooking steaks and doing a great job. Then he came to me and asked if we had a fire extinguisher. I thought, 'Here's a dedicated guy.' I said, 'Here's the big fire bottle' and he took it and ran outside because he had set the building on fire! But we didn't have to evacuate and he got the fire out in a hurry.*[219]

Radomes, pictured at Montauk Air Force Base, Camp Hero, in 1957, were weatherproof enclosures that protected radar equipment from the effects of the elements. Jim Sullivan was stationed at the base 1957-1958. (Jim Sullivan photo)

In 1958 a SAGE radar system was installed at the Montauk Air Force Station and the facility was merged into the SAGE national air defense network. Part of the equipment included a huge AN/FPS-35 radar antenna, built by Sperry Gyroscope at Lake Success, Long Island. It was installed in 1960. Since the Sperry plant was only about 100 miles from Montauk, it is thought that this antenna was the first one built in the country.

The antenna "dish," standing atop an 80-foot tall, 30-ton concrete base, was 126-feet long and 38-feet wide, weighing approximately 40 tons, and could detect aircraft at distances of over 250 miles. It measured 160 feet from top to ground. Radar data collected was sent to the SAGE Direction Center at McGuire Air Force Base in New Jersey. This advanced Specific Frequency Diversity Search Radar operated until the station shut down in 1981.

Jim Sullivan explained the range of the radar:

> It was augmented by airborne early warning aircraft that flew out of Otis [Air Force Base at Falmouth, MA]. They had radar aboard with a range of about 150 miles which extended your range, which gave you time to get out and ID an aircraft before it got too close…

> The site was also augmented by Texas tower-type sites in the Atlantic, and Navy blimps that flew about 1000 feet above the ocean. Those Texas towers didn't last too long since they couldn't survive the ocean waves and currents.[220]

The AN/FPS-35 was one of the first four of its type built in the United States, others being at air force bases in Thomasville, Alabama, Benton, Pennsylvania, and Manassas, Virginia. Eventually, twelve were built across the country.

Although the site was run by the Air Force, the actual radar equipment was run and maintained by Sperry workers.

According to Dick White, the radar operators stationed at the Air Force Station "sat and looked at radar screens, like television sets, in a dark room. They were referred to as 'scope dopes.'"[221]

No sooner was the antenna put in service when, in 1961, it was taken out of service due to the significant electrical interference it generated, affecting local radio and television reception. The problem was corrected and the system was up and running again in 1962.

Vinnie Grimes recalled those days when the "big monster [antenna] drove us nuts. Every time it went around you'd get snow on the TV. And that sucker would wait until the guy [on television] was headin' for a touchdown and there would come the snow! We spent fortunes on TV's; switched from Sylvania to RCA, but same damned thing happened, no matter what TV you got. That antenna was powerful."[222]

Dick White echoed these thoughts: "You could set your watch by it. Any electronic device, like a radio, alarm clock, was affected. After a while, you didn't hear it."[223]

The Montauk facility became a major part of the NORAD (North American Aerospace Defense Command) defense system, and security was extremely tight. The unit was renamed the 773rd Radar Squadron in 1963. That year it became a joint FAA and Air Force site, with data used by the FAA for air traffic control and by the Air Force for air defense operations. The base reverted to its original purpose of providing only air defense radar coverage for the region in 1965.

In December 1963 it was announced that for economic reasons the Army planned to relocate some

Hercules anti-aircraft missiles to Camp Hero from Fort Tilden on Rockaway Point, New York, and these would be in place by December 1966. Though it could have required up to a hundred military personnel and additional civilian employees, providing an economic boost for Montauk, the plan was squelched in August 1965. One of the reasons was that the Nike installation required an area about 1,500-feet wide south of the Point to be off limits to private boating, an area considered "one of the most productive fishing areas on which Montauk can boast."[224]

During 1967, the SAGE center at McGuire Air Force base was deactivated and data was then sent to the SAGE center at Hancock Field in Syracuse, New York.

Major Robert W. Zarn, one time commander of the 773rd Radar Squadron, spoke of life at the base in 1967:

> Because the area is primarily a resort one, rents are quite high, sometimes higher than our airmen can really afford. Outside of that we have no major problems.
>
> We work closely with the local church groups, particularly Rev. Friend in Montauk. It is a little bleak here in the winter for our single airmen, but we have movies on the base three times a week, plus gym equipment and a hobby shop and another shop where they can work on their cars. A surprising number of our airmen come from this area.[225]

Bruce McAuliffe of Medina, Ohio (born 1930), was stationed at Miller Field at Fort Wadsworth, Staten Island, New York in 1954. He noted that every so often he was part of a contingent of men assigned to assemble and transport 90mm weapons out to Camp Hero. They would set up for a two-week period of firing at targets consisting of either a sleeve towed by a plane or floating devices towed by picket boats. He worked as a message center clerk while at the base.

On one occasion, McAuliffe recalled that a general was coming to inspect the base. "The star meant something," he said, so the men at the base did their best to prepare for the general's arrival. As the time drew near, it was discovered that a particular jeep was filthy and dirty. "When the question was put to the sergeant-major as to how best and fastest to clean it he told us, 'Use your imagination,' so we ran the jeep into the ocean. It had a snorkel on it so the engine would run while it was underwater. It came out a little waterlogged, but a lot cleaner than it had been before!"

McAuliffe said, "Waking up on weekends and hearing the foghorn [at the lighthouse], and hearing the waves roll in, were some of my most memorable thoughts of being at Montauk. Those sounds were the 'Rolling Stones' of Montauk!' "[226]

Byron Lindsey (born 1930) of St. Marie, Montana, was stationed at the Air Force Base from 1969-1971. He said of the huge antenna, "We called it the 'big pig'." It contained giant-sized radar and had marvelous capabilities. It couldn't be jammed by anybody. It had random pulsing so nobody could log on to it. It was very effective, had five megawatts. It was a big monster, everything was large on it. It took six 100 horsepower engines to turn that antenna."

When asked if he recalled any humorous incidents while stationed at Montauk, he replied, "That big antenna had a big bearing ring that the antenna turned around on which was under tenuous pressure and had to be lubricated constantly. The oil they used migrated very good, so we ordered Kotex by the case to absorb the oil. We listed Kotex as one of our maintenance items."

According to Lindsey, housing was in short supply in those years: "When I first moved in there I was

Senior Master Sergeant and moved into base housing. I had some other guys come in and they needed housing, but the nearest place they could get was fifty miles away. So I figured, being in charge, I didn't have to be there. The men doing the maintenance had to be on site. I had a house down in Riverhead so I stayed there. Once in a while I stayed in the barracks on site. Actually, Flanders was the closest place where men could rent. Eventually we had carpooling."[227] The sentiment toward the military presence at Camp Hero warmed over the years, as reflected in a letter from the Town of East Hampton to newly arriving airmen in 1974:

*Welcome to Montauk. Whether you are an old friend or a newcomer, we are glad you are here.*

*There are many things we love about East Hampton Town: Its clear air and virgin woods, its bays and harbors, its wildlife and marine life, its open farms, white beaches, and rolling dunes. We feel that it is a privilege to live here and we welcome you to share the bounties of our community life.*

*The Montauk Air Force Station has become an integral part of this town and the people of East Hampton want your stay here to be happy one. Please do not hesitate to call upon me and other members of the Town Board if we may be of service.*

*Sincerely, Judith Hope, Supervisor*[228]

Overgrown by the forces of nature, the two 16-inch gun emplacements of Battery 112 are still visible in this 1985 view. Today, descriptive plaques are scattered about, explaining the function of this and other equipment at Camp Hero. (Marge Winski photo)

Ralph William (Bill) Conant (born 1936), of Arcadia, Florida, was the officer in charge at the Coast Guard station at nearby Montauk Point Lighthouse from 1971-1975. He noted some of the activities that went on at Camp Hero:

> *Sometimes they would have alerts. The base was closed down, but we were always notified by phone. There were a lot of National Guard troops that would train on the base. They repelled on the cliffs as part of their training. Every summer we had that type of thing going on.*

> *Sometimes, they would play their war games at night and they would come to us and ask if they could use the fire control tower. They would get on top of that and use their night-spotting scopes to keep track of troop movements in the brush.*[229]

A scary situation developed in October 1975 when a four-foot tear was discovered in the giant bubble housing the height-finding radar transmitter. Technicians came up with the solution: "The bubble was pressurized, and air was leaking out slowly but surely…The pressure was allowed to drop, and when the bubble had collapsed, the hole, along a seam, was sewn up. It is now said to be as good as new."[230]

There also were humorous incidents at Camp Hero such as the following:

> *A young soldier was bedecked with jewelry one evening by an infatuated East Hampton woman. On his return to Fort Hero, he was afraid it would be stolen, so he hid his presents in the innards of a radar transmitter. A short-circuit ensured, shutting down the operation for eight hours. At his court martial it developed that he was only 15, and he was sent home, minus the jewelry.*[231]

During the days of the Air Force Station, military personnel had a 1:00a.m. curfew that caused a few vehicular accidents along the portion of the Montauk Highway known as the "Napeague Stretch" by men trying to beat it.

In May 1978 the Air Force submitted a proposal to close the base, since advances in satellite technology basically rendered the facility obsolete. An angry New York Assemblyman, Perry Duryea (1921-2004) of Montauk voiced his opinion on the decision:

> *I am concerned about our national security and the direction the [President Jimmy] Carter administration is taking that security. But I am equally concerned about the loss of 110 military personnel, and the loss of the jobs of 30 civilian personnel at the Montauk Air Force Station. I will urge our Congressional delegation in Washington to seek to have the President reverse this decision.*[232]

Conversely, Suffolk County, New York Congressman Otis G. Pike (1921- ) was not upset about the closing of the Air Force Station:

Seen in December 2005, Battery 113 and the radar antenna are part of what military buffs, as well as hikers and curiosity seekers, can see within Camp Hero State Park. Descriptive plaques display historic facts and images about the days when the base was a coastal defense stronghold. (Author photo)

*If it has outlived its usefulness, I am not going to lead the charge to try to keep it in operation. A military program should not ever be justified on the basis of how many jobs it creates, but only on the basis of what it can contribute to the national defense.*[233]

Base commander Major Michael Hoskins said the radar itself was not technically obsolete, but the Air Force program planning to combine its radar installations with those run by the FAA would make the Montauk operation unnecessary.[234]

When Major Miles Martin arrived as the base's last commander in July 1978, there were 120 military and civilian workers left. Over the next two years the number dwindled down.

In June 1980 it was announced that in the coming weeks the station was to shut down and the radar antenna, which had been rotating once every twelve seconds since 1962, would be removed and disassembled. The Town of East Hampton looked to acquire the land containing 27 houses for low- and moderate-income housing, while the State looked to add parkland to its already ample park holdings on the Montauk Peninsula.

The new radar system operated by the FAA was activated in Riverhead on July 1, 1980 and Montauk officially shut down its radar operation. The new system could handle both civilian and air defense requirements, thus making the SAGE system redundant. Major Martin held a base-closing ceremony in November, while there were still enough personnel left to hold the ceremony.

The 773rd Radar Squadron at the Air Force Base shut down on January 31, 1981. Being very large and difficult to remove, it was decided that the huge antenna would be "abandoned in place;" its controlling mechanism and electronics removed so it could move with the wind to prevent it being damaged in a severe storm. All radars were removed, except a GATR (Ground Air Transmitter Receiver), which remained to direct military aircraft operating in the region. This, too, was deactivated and removed in 1984. Today, the antenna and the Montauk Point Lighthouse serve jointly as daymarks for vessels at sea.

In 1982, 138 acres of Camp Hero were deeded to New York State by the Department of Defense. In 1983 the General Services Administration transferred 30 acres containing 27 residences to the Town of East Hampton to be sold as moderate-income housing.

During 1984 remaining portions of the military reservation were donated to the National Park Service, which turned it over to the State of New York. Certain sections not considered environmentally sensitive were sold. A total of 415 acres were transferred to the State.

During the years between the shutdown and the opening of Camp Hero State Park in 2002, Preston Nichols and Peter Moon wrote a book in 1992 entitled *The Montauk Project: Experiments in Time*, in which they claimed that top secret experiments were conducted at Camp Hero involving psychological warfare, time travel, invisibility, even contact with aliens! While the book and subsequent publications proved popular with science fiction fans, none of these claims have been substantiated.

Park superintendent Tom Dess hoped that once the park opened it would put these tales to rest, but it didn't. People who were associated with the base refused to answer reporters' questions unless they were assured that their responses would not give validity to what one called, "some hokey UFO / mind-control / government-conspiracy / time-travel nonsense."[235]

As part of the cleanup of Camp Hero, the Army Corps of Engineers removed toxic debris and unexploded munitions on the property and, in 2000, tore down several buildings that were part of the "fishing village" built by the Army during World War II.

Camp Hero State Park opened to the public on September 18, 2002. A network of trails runs through the park, among them the "old" Old Montauk Highway that once was the only road to the Point. Along the way are scenic vistas, and signs of nature. Among the remaining buildings in what was the "downtown" area of the camp, is the gymnasium building, disguised to resemble a church. It is the only original remaining structure. Batteries 112 and 113 can be seen, though now walled up completely to prevent vandalism in the interior.

The huge radar "dish" remains the centerpiece, though inaccessible. There were plans to develop a museum focusing on WWII and the Cold War in the structure beneath the monster antenna, but to date no progress has been made in that direction. A walk along the eroded cliffs affords spectacular views of the Atlantic Ocean and the Montauk Point Lighthouse, located about a mile to the east. For the history or nature buff, a visit to Camp Hero will stir the imagination in what has become a seemingly magical and haunting place.

Disguised as a church, this building housed the gymnasium for military personnel. It is the only remaining original building from the World War II era at Camp Hero. The photo was taken in 2005. (Author photo)

Pictured are the wartime army barracks that were located in the "downtown" section of Camp Hero. The photo was taken in December 2005. (Author photo)

Looming ominously over the trees, the AN/FPS-35 Radar Antenna, photographed in December 2005, is today the centerpiece of Camp Hero State Park and a symbol of a bygone era in radar technology. (Author photo)

# CHAPTER 10

# The United States Coast Guard

WHILE NOT EXCLUSIVE to Montauk's military story, the presence of the U. S. Coast Guard (USCG) has been a part of Montauk history since the establishment of the Coast Guard's predecessors, the U. S. Life Saving Service (USLSS), the U.S. Lighthouse Service, and the U.S. Revenue Cutter Service. A Coast Guard presence would eventually encompass all three entities and their missions.

The Revenue Cutter Service had been established in 1790 to enforce tariff and maritime laws and prevent smuggling. In 1837 Congress authorized it also to look for shipwrecks, save lives, and property, and destroy abandoned vessels at sea. The Lighthouse Service, which began in 1789, was tasked with providing guidance along coasts and waterways and preventing shipwrecks. In the event maritime disasters occurred, the Life Saving Service, begun in 1848 and formalized in 1871, would see to the needs of vessels and mariners in distress.

The Revenue Cutter Service and Life Saving Service were combined in 1915 to form the U.S. Coast Guard. In 1939, the Lighthouse Service also was added to the Coast Guard mission. Two other agencies—the Steamboat Inspection Service and the Bureau of Navigation—came under Coast Guard jurisdiction in 1942.

The life saving effort was somewhat informal at first and originated on Long Island in 1849 when eight small stations were constructed along the South Shore. Because of the dangerous barrier beaches located only a quarter of a mile offshore, many a vessel found itself aground there in fog-shrouded calm waters as well as from dangerous storms. The closest station to Montauk at that time was at Amagansett, about ten miles west of the heart of the Montauk Peninsula. During these early years no provision was made for permanent or salaried keepers. Responsibility for any equipment usually fell to the most responsible person living nearest to the station.

The Montauk Peninsula eventually had three life saving stations. In 1854 property was conveyed for a station at Ditch Plains, about three and a half miles west of Montauk Point Lighthouse, and a station was built the following year. Former Montauk Lighthouse keeper Patrick Gould (1799-1879) was appointed first keeper.

Even though a bill was passed in 1854 to provide for additional stations along the shores of Long Island and New Jersey, and also for paid keepers, there was a lack of effective discipline and control which gave the service a bad reputation.

Weather conditions could be rough at times on Montauk. A lightning strike destroyed the station in March 1891 and it burned down, but it was rebuilt. The station's boathouse was destroyed in the hurricane of September 21, 1938. Station Ditch Plains was open through World War II and was still operating in 1945. The station was no longer listed as active as of 1956.

A life saving station existed at Ditch Plain from 1855 until after WW II. The 1885 station (pictured) was destroyed by a lightning strike in 1891 and replaced. The crew appears ready to roll in this ca.1890 image. (Montauk Point Lighthouse Museum)

In 1855 land was set aside for another life saving station at Hither Plain, five and a half miles west of the lighthouse and half a mile south of Fort Pond. A building was not constructed there until 1871.

Somewhat of a mystery is the station at Montauk Point. Located right at the Point by the lighthouse, no land was conveyed and no structure built for a station. What is known is the following statement in the 1878 Annual Report of the U. S. Life Saving Service: "The new station mentioned as desirable to be built at Montauk Point has not been erected, it being found impossible to obtain title to the site selected on account of the premises being in litigation." By 1900 it was listed as "in charge of keeper of Ditch Plains Station; no crew employed."[238] The first keeper assigned to the Montauk life saving station was believed to be Jonathan Miller, who at the time was also keeper of the lighthouse.

The original service was all-volunteer, consisting mostly of farmers and fishermen who made the system work for them by having summers off to pursue their trades. Most life saving duties were needed during the colder months, when storms were more of a problem.

The service was reorganized and officially named the United States Life Saving Service in 1871 by Sumner Kimball (1834-1923). Under his leadership, many improvements were made, such as employing qualified surfmen with pay at all stations during months when they were most needed, instituting beach patrols, and providing self-bailing rowboats and other lifesaving equipment. He drew up regulations with standards of performance for crew members. In the early 1890s, crews were off from May 1st to September 1st each year, but by 1898 they were on duty ten months out of the year. The station keeper, however, was on duty year round.

Under the new system, stations were referred to by number: Montauk Point #6, Ditch Plain #7,

Ditch Plain Life Saving Station presents a tidy appearance in this image from August 1913. Note the tower where a watch was kept twenty-four hours a day and the ramp for rolling out the surfboat and other equipment. (Montauk Point Lighthouse Museum)

Hither Plain #8, etc. About 1890 they were referred to by name. In 1889 a government telephone system connected all stations from Montauk to Rockaway Point in Queens. During the Spanish-American War, several stations were commissioned as Coast Signal Stations, with crews on the lookout for enemy vessels.

In all, more than thirty life saving stations were built about five miles apart from each other from Montauk to the Rockaway Peninsula. Long Island was considered one of the most dangerous coasts in the nation and saw heavy shipping traffic, due to the proximity of large ports; thus, its stations were many in number and closely situated. Cape Cod, the Outer Banks, and New Jersey had near-equal need for many life saving stations, but elsewhere in the nation the stations were spaced much farther apart. On the West Coast, for example, there were sometimes gaps of 50 to 100 miles between life saving stations.

Everett King (1866-1947) of East Hampton said back then of the new system:

> *Every man had to be as good a surfman as the other. Each one of us had to take his turn being captain. We had to put the boats in once a week. During World War I when I was at Hither Plain Station they sent us two sailors as replacements. Neither one had ever handled an oar or seen the ocean before… The first time a sea kicked up, one boy just lay down on the beach and looked at it. 'I couldn't even go off through those waves,' he said. 'I didn't know water even got like that.'*[237]

Under Sumner Kimball's system, Station Hither Plain was built in 1871 with George H. Osborne appointed as first keeper. The station remained in service until 1934. To aid in coastline defense it was reactivated during World War II and finally abandoned in 1948. The station was torn down in later years.

The United States entered World War II the day after what President Franklin Roosevelt called the "dastardly attack" by Japanese forces on Pearl Harbor on December 7, 1941. Japan's Axis allies, Germany and Italy, followed suit by declaring war on the United States on December 11th. This set the stage for German submarines called "U boats" to begin their onslaught against allied shipping off America's east coast. Only five weeks after entering the war against the Axis Powers, on January 14, 1942, the U-123, captained by Reinhard Hardegen (1913-), torpedoed the Panamanian ship *Norness* about 60 miles southeast of Montauk Point. This was the first of over 100 ships to be torpedoed (mostly between Cape Cod and Cape Hatteras) off America's east coast over the first six months of the year.

The Coast Guard was pressed into service, watching for enemy submarine activity. Grim reminders of war were often found washed ashore in the form of life preservers, life rafts, and other fragments from torpedoed vessels. Dick White, though quite young at the time, has "vivid memories of seeing stuff on the beach of ships that had been blown apart."[238]

In the past, Coast Guard personnel carried flashlights, Coston signals (flares), and time clocks when on patrol. During the war they carried guns. This change was a result of an event that took place at Amagansett, Long Island in June 1942, which put the Coast Guard on the front page of newspapers around the nation and shocked Americans, since it involved a breach of our security during time of war.

Coast Guard installations existed at the lighthouse, Ditch Plains, and Hither Plain on Montauk. According to John Ecker (born 1925), formerly of Montauk and now of East Hampton, the Hither Plain station was on the south side of Old Montauk Highway across from the present Surfside Inn east of Washington Drive. Ecker, whose family moved to Montauk from Pennsylvania in 1936, lived in the old fishing village and witnessed the destruction caused by the 1938 hurricane and the actions of the Navy in removing what was left of the quaint village on Fort Pond Bay.

A dirigible cruises by the Hither Plain Life Saving Station on Montauk in 1917. (Montauk Point Lighthouse Museum)

A view of Old Montauk Highway in May 1924 looks east toward Hither Plain Life Saving Station. (Queens Borough Public Library, Long Island Division, Eugene L. Armbruster Photographs)

He explained that the Coast Guard dredged Montauk Harbor deeper to accommodate their fleet of auxiliary patrol boats. These vessels were yachts, owned by civilians, who turned them over to the Coast Guard for use on their patrols to look for U-boats. Auxiliary boats were also kept at the Yacht Club on Star Island in Lake Montauk.[239]

Milton Miller spoke in August 2010 about his service in the Coast Guard during the war:

*I entered the service in 1938 and put two years in at the Ditch Plains Coast Guard Station from 1941 to 1942. In stormy, foggy weather we'd walk the cliffs from the station to the lighthouse. After four hours the pickup would meet us there and bring us back to Ditch Plains. But there was always somebody on watch at the lighthouse.*

*They didn't have a patrol boat. They didn't have nothin'. We used Howard Johnson's yacht; the guy that owned the restaurants. She was 60-foot. It looked like at PT boat. Later I was transferred to a regular PT boat.*

*We could report the location of a[n enemy] submarine but couldn't take no action on 'em. We had to go through the Navy, which took over the Coast Guard, and what a mess that was! Every time we saw something we had to call the base. Ours was Lakeland Air Force Base in New Jersey. If they had any problem they would call Sandy Hook. They would do about twenty different things before you could take action.*

*While I was at Ditch Plains, in January 1942 two tankers were sunk; one off Block Island and one off Shinnecock. I went out on both of them. I was in charge of the rescue operation. We had two self-righting lifeboats. The [Montauk] Yacht Club on Star Island was turned into a base. They must have had fifteen patrol boats in there.*

*I got on a patrol boat and I was doing patrol duty from Block Island to Sandy Hook. When I was transferred they hadn't started on building Fort (Camp) Hero. It wasn't even thought about then.*[240]

Milton Miller (middle row, far left) posed with the crew at the Ditch Plains Coast Guard Station in 1941. Miller was stationed here 1941-1942 before going overseas. (Courtesy of Milton Miller)

Ever ready to respond to those in peril at sea, the crew of Amagansett Life Saving Station is seen at a more leisurely moment in 1902. The station was where John Cullen was stationed on that fateful night in June 1942 when four Nazi saboteurs came ashore nearby. (Montauk Point Lighthouse Museum)

In 1942 Miller was transferred to the war in the Pacific Theatre where he took part in many campaigns against Japanese forces. On February 23, 1945 he witnessed one of the most historic moments of the war—the planting of the American flag atop Mount Suribachi on the island of Iwo Jima.

Amagansett, a Hamptons hamlet located only about ten miles west of Montauk village, was a quiet place in early June of 1942. Still too early for the summer crowds, it lay patiently awaiting the arrival of vacationers.

By June 1942, "Operation Paukenschlog" (Drumbeat), the German U-boat campaign masterminded by German Admiral Karl Donitz (1891-1980), had sunk nearly a half million tons of shipping and taken about 2,000 lives in the process. With a vast array of U-boats blanketing the Atlantic, one of them, the *U-202*, was able to slither its way through a thick fog on the night of June 13, 1942 to within a half mile of Long Island's East End. The mission was sabotage.

The story begins at Quentz Farm, the German School of Sabotage. Created by German Military Intelligence and located about 40 miles west of Berlin, the school was to train agents in the art of sabotage. Upon completion, "graduates" were to infiltrate the United States and destroy vital power plants, factories, and communications. Eight men were chosen for the mission, split into two four-man teams. All eight had spent time in the United States and were familiar with the language and customs.

The project was given the name, "Operation Pastorius," named for Francis Daniel Pastorius (1651-1720) who founded Germantown, Pennsylvania in 1683, the first German settlement in America.

The two teams were to be transported to the east coast of Long Island via submarine *U-202*, under the command of Kapitanleutnant (equivalent to the U. S. Navy rank of lieutenant) Hans-Heinz Linder (1913-1944). Team leader George John Dasch (1903-1992) was aboard, along with three others. Another submarine, the *U- 584*, took the other four to Ponte Vedra Beach near Jacksonville, Florida.

The plan was to destroy hydroelectric plants belonging to the Aluminium Company of America at Niagara Falls, New York, and factories and locks on the Ohio River, blow up Pennsylvania Station at Newark, New Jersey, attack locks and canal installations at St Louis, Missouri, and attempt to destroy the New York City water supply. It was quite a task for just eight men!

Just after midnight on Saturday, June 13, 1942, young 2nd class Coast Guard Seaman John C. Cullen (born 1920), set out on beach patrol from the Amagansett Coast Guard Station, armed only with a flashlight and flare gun. He was accustomed to this detail, having done it for a couple of months. Usually, he would find nothing and see no one. But this night would be dramatically different. What follows is his story, given in a Coast Guard interview in 2006 with Dr. William Thiesen, a Coast Guard historian.

Cullen started walking in fog so thick he couldn't see his shoes. He proceeded to walk about 20-30 minutes from the Coast Guard Station and spotted two individuals talking at the water's edge. Cullen watched them from a safe distance. Finally, he moved closer and called out to them. They turned around, and one of them said, "You Coast Guard?" Cullen replied, "Yes, I am. What are you doing here?" The man said, "We were fishing and our boat ran aground, and we're going to stay here until daybreak."

The man who had spoken with Cullen turned around and walked to the other man. He returned shortly and said to Cullen, "Look, you got a mother and father?" Cullen replied, "Yeah. What's that got to do with it?" The stranger's retort: "Well, it's best that you don't know too much. You just do what we tell you, and everything will be fine. You got a mother and father, and you want to see them again."

There was another man in back of Cullen in the sand dunes who came up dragging a sea bag and speaking in German. He said to the fellow that Cullen was talking with, "Shut up, and get down with the others." It was then that Cullen realized these men were Germans. He wondered what they were doing on the shore in the darkness.

It was later determined that there were four men on the beach that night, and two were burying explosives in the sand dunes. The man, later identified as George John Dasch, told Cullen, "We'll give you money, and you forget about this." Cullen, looking to get away with his life, said, "Okay, it's a deal." Dasch handed him what was supposed to be $300.

Cullen noticed a strong odor of diesel fuel in the air, which was unusual.

Dasch said to Cullen, "Look in my face. Will you recognize me again if you saw me?" Quick-thinking Cullen replied, "No, I never saw you before. I don't know you."

Cullen later told an interviewer, "I backed away slowly up to the sand dunes and ran like hell for the station. I didn't trust them. I didn't think I was going to get out of there."

When he returned to the Coast Guard Station, he turned over the money to Officer Carl Jenette, who was in charge. It was discovered that there was only $260 in cash. Station CO Warren Barnes, who lived in East Hampton, was notified by telephone. A short time later, four officers including Cullen, armed with rifles, returned to the beach.

Said Cullen: "We spread out. We thought whoever was there might still be there." It was then they heard the rumble from the submarine. According to Cullen, "There was a blinker light from the sub. We knew it was a surface vessel because of the blinker light, and we figured it was a submarine because the beach vibrated. Remember there was a tide, and it was stuck on a sand dune."

Nothing was found, so they went out again at dawn, this time in the company of Army and Navy personnel. The FBI also showed up and immediately took charge of the investigation. After looking for the area where the confrontation occurred, Cullen found a package of German cigarettes.

The saboteurs were nowhere to be found. The previous night, after encountering Cullen, the four men had headed north on Atlantic Avenue to Montauk Highway and made their way to the Amagansett station of the Long Island Railroad. There, they boarded the 6:57 a.m. train to New York, according to plan.

The FBI wanted to speak with Cullen and immediately took him to the home of an FBI agent in East Hampton. Cullen said, "There, they interviewed me, asked me question after question. They figured I must be part of this, that if they are who they are, you're not going to survive, but I was lucky. And then I told them, one after the other, this is what happened, and they were shocked."

As far as the recovery of the explosives, Cullen pointed out, "It was a Naval intelligence officer that was there, and the Coast Guard was there. And they are the ones that found it." He said the spot was marked by a pair of German bathing trunks.

Cullen described the handling of the explosives: "Four cases of incendiary bombs were brought into the boathouse. Fortunately, the Coast Guard had an officer there who came out, and he said, 'Well, open it up and see what's in here, but be careful.' So he did. He opened it up and there was a five-gallon can full of excelsior [long, thin wood shavings used for packing], and there were different types of bombs, pieces of coal, fountain pens. You open it, and it would explode."

The Coast Guardsman packed the items back in the excelsior, and took them to the Coast Guard in New York. Cullen noted that, "The Coast Guard got in trouble for taking that, and it should have went to

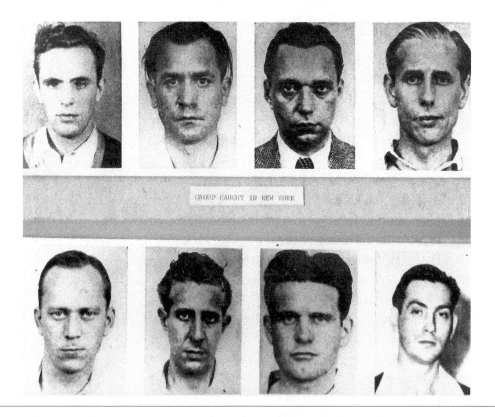

GROUP CAUGHT IN NEW YORK

These eight Nazi saboteurs were captured in June 1942. Those that landed at Amagansett, Long Island were (top row, left to right): Herbert Haupt, Werner Thiel, Ernest Burger, George Dasch. Those that landed at Ponte Vedra Beach, Florida were (bottom row, left to right): Heinrich Heinck, Richard Quirin, Edward Kerling, Hermann Neubauer. (Montauk Point Lighthouse Museum)

Legion of Merit winner, Coast Guardsman John C. Cullen,
Boatswain's Mate first class.

John Cullen, 2nd Class Seaman, USCG, was awarded the Legion of Merit for his prompt actions after discovering the Nazi landing at Amagansett on June 15, 1942. (Montauk Point Lighthouse Museum)

the FBI, but the FBI went there and got it. Unfortunately, the Coast Guard didn't get the recognition that they should have. It was mostly FBI. J. Edgar Hoover. He wanted the credit for it."[241]

While all of this was happening on Long Island, the other submarine, *U-584*, landed at Ponte Vedra Beach, Florida on June 16th. Off they went by train to Chicago and Cincinnati to start their mission of destruction.

Meanwhile, the Long Island group had reached New York. Once there, the leader of the operation, George Dasch, who all along had planned to sabotage not the United States but the mission itself so he could return to America, convinced one of his group members, Ernest Burgher, to go along with the idea. Dasch raced to Washington D.C., and turned himself in to the FBI, informing them of the entire plot. Within two weeks it was all over; the FBI had all eight men in custody. They were brought to trial before a Military Commission on July 8th in the Department of Justice Building in Washington. All were found guilty and given the death penalty.

In an interview in April 2010, John Cullen's wife Alice (John was suffering from dementia and unfortunately recalled nothing of the event) pointed out that "before the trial began Dasch requested to speak with John first and authorities allowed that. Dasch said to John, 'Remember, I had orders to kill you.'" She said that Dasch's request infuriated J. Edgar Hoover, and immediately after John testified he was sent back to Long Island, presumably because Hoover did not want him to be the center of attention, and his absence from the proceedings would give the FBI the chance to take all the credit for the capture of the Germans.[242]

Because Dasch and Burgher had cooperated with authorities, President Franklin Roosevelt commuted Burgher's sentence to life and Dasch's to 30 years. The other six were all put to death by electrocution on August 8th. In 1948, President Harry Truman granted clemency to Dasch and Burgher, and they were deported to the U.S. Occupied Zone in West Germany.

George Dasch had been "promised" a full pardon by J. Edgar Hoover for his part in exposing the plot, thus enabling him to stay in the United States, which was Dasch's goal in the first place. That pardon never came, even after Hoover's death in 1972. Dasch moved from place to place and job to job for many years. He died in 1992 at the age of 89, still waiting for some word that would clear his name in American history.

John Cullen was awarded the Legion of Merit by the Coast Guard for his prompt action in reporting the landing of the German saboteurs and was promoted to coxswain. The award to Cullen is described as follows:

> *For exceptionally meritorious conduct while on patrol at Long Island, New York, on the night of June 13, 1942. When several Nazi saboteurs bearing boxes of TNT and other destructive apparatus landed on the beach at Amagansett Cullen, unarmed and helpless against their menacing threat cleverly allayed their suspicions and thwarted their subversive intentions by promptly accepting a proffered bribe then sounding an alarm that led to their eventual capture. Subsequently volunteering as member of a searching party, he remained on the beach all night and after apprehension of the enemy agents. Furnished vital and incriminating testimony before a special military commission conducting trial. His keen presence of mind and discerning judgment in a grave emergency undoubtedly prevented the successful culmination of hostile intrigue designed to sabotage our national war effort.*[243]

John Cullen was transferred from Amagansett to Ellis Island in New York and later to a Coast Guard transportation center, which was located across the street from Ebbets Field in Brooklyn. Alice Cullen noted, "He got to see [Brooklyn Dodgers baseball] games once in a while. They treated him very well over there." She and John married in 1944. Since John was still in the service he had to get married in uniform.

Alice said that John became suspicious of the men on the beach when they claimed they were out looking for clams. "You didn't get clams from the ocean. That, and the fact they were speaking in German really made John suspicious."

Archie Jones was OIC (officer in charge) at the Montauk Point Lighthouse when the Coast Guard took over operations there in 1946. He served until 1954. (Montauk Point Lighthouse)

Archie Jones is pictured heading for the top of the lighthouse at Montauk Point, ca. 1950. (Montauk Point Lighthouse Museum)

Alice said John was always very modest about the incident with the German saboteurs. "He was very blasé about it and would only talk about it if someone asked him to. He would say anyone would have done what he did under the circumstances and it just so happened to be him that night. He didn't do anything out of the ordinary. He did what he had to do."[244]

"New recruits [to the Coast Guard] were coming about every day," said Milton Miller of East Hampton, who also joined their ranks and was stationed at Ditch Plains, Montauk for a period of time. "They were ready and willing to join the service to protect the nation and its people. John Cullen was one of these people. He did what had to be done."[245]

After the war, in 1946, the Coast Guard took over operation of the Montauk Point Lighthouse. The era of the civilian keeper at Montauk Point actually ended in 1943 when the Army took over the lighthouse for the duration of the war. Now that peace had returned, former President Franklin Roosevelt's 1939 declaration that all navigational aids in the country would be under Coast Guard control took effect at Montauk.

The first OIC at the lighthouse was Archie Jones, who served until 1954. Jones was from Marshallberg, North Carolina. (It was not unusual for many Coast Guard officers up north to be from "down Hatteras way" in those days.) After the hectic days of the war, the Coast Guard years at the lighthouse were calm by comparison. However, the lighthouse station was maintained efficiently, contributing to the safe passage of vessels sailing past the Point.

Another OIC at Montauk was Ira Lewis (born 1918), who served 1957-1959. He grew up on Harkers Island, North Carolina and enlisted with the Coast Guard in 1938. In an interview with his son Phil in February 2010 (Ira is 92 and hard of hearing) , Phil spoke of life at the lighthouse back when he was about 12-14 years old. The family originally lived in Center Moriches, Long Island until Ira was assigned to Montauk. Phil recalled visiting the lighthouse in 1955 when Charles Schumacher was the OIC. The

Archie Jones and family enjoy a quiet moment at Montauk Lighthouse, ca.1950. The Coast Guard years at Montauk were calm as compared to the hectic times of the war years before. (Montauk Point Lighthouse Museum)

Lewises came out one day with camping equipment and pitched their tent behind the garage. "There was good fishing out there," said Phil, "and Charlie would take us out."

Phil recalled that on Armed Forces Day (the third Saturday of May), Camp Hero held an open house and people were given tours of the radar dome. "Once in a while we'd even see a blimp go by," he added. He also remembered Archie Jones because Archie's sister was one of Phil's teachers. In addition, Phil's sister Margaret married Archie's granddaughter.[246]

The Montauk Point Lighthouse Museum has several photos donated by Ira Lewis a few years ago that depict the activities at the site, including the arduous task of whitewashing the tower. During the summer of 1957 Ira and his crew painted the entire tower from top to bottom.

Several other Coast Guard officers managed the Light Station until the light and fog signal were automated on February 3, 1987. One of them, Ralph William (Bill) Conant, of Arcadia, Florida, was the officer in charge from 1971-1975. He noted that the biggest event during that time was the restoration of the bluff around the lighthouse, spearheaded by Giorgina Reid, a professional photographer, who began terracing the bluff around the lighthouse in 1970:

> They started the gabions when I was there. They were installed from fence to fence on Coast Guard property. My son worked with the crew that put them in. My family worked with Giorgina. She would come out on the weekend. I had a pickup camper and I invited her and her husband Donald to stay in the camper right there on the base when they came out. She was real thrilled about that.
>
> Dick Cavett was there quite a bit. He had the same problem on his property [nearby] and Giorgina worked with him a couple of times, too, showing him how to fix the erosion problem.

Enlisting in the Coast Guard in 1938, Ira Lewis served at a number of Long Island stations. He was the OIC at Montauk from March 1957 (pictured) until his retirement on August 1, 1959. Now 92, Lewis lives in North Carolina. (Ira Lewis Collection, (Montauk Point Lighthouse Museum)

*Giorgina was an interesting person. She was also a freelance photographer and she must have developed a thousand pictures for me. Any picture I took she critiqued, telling me what I should have done. We gave her a Coast Guard hard hat with her name on the back. Well, you would think we had given her a great prize because she wore that thing with pride any time she was out there. She and Donald were very special people.*

*A lot of times Giorgina would come out by train and we would pick her up at the Montauk train station. She'd get out there about noontime and work for four or five hours, then catch the late train back into the city. She was quite dedicated. My two youngest kids helped her by bringing bundles of reeds and she'd get them out there working on the bluff. All of the guys liked her and would do anything for her, including picking her up from and bring her to the train station.*

Conant said his men also had a good relationship with the personnel stationed at the air force base in Camp Hero, located adjacent to the lighthouse property:

*We had a gate down by the garage between our property and theirs so we wouldn't have to go out to the road. It was large enough to drive a car through. Our kids would ride their bikes through there to the air force property. They also used to play in the old bunker all the time; crawl in through the gun slits in front of it.*

Conant noted some changes made at the lighthouse station during his time there:

*They hadn't had access to the property by school groups for a number of years. We opened it up to school tours. We must have had more than a thousand kids come out. We had them every week and it was a lot of fun doing that. We believed it was part of their local history and they should have the opportunity to see it. We didn't always take them up into the tower. Most of the time, we did.*

*We sometimes opened the property up on weekends for tours, but if it got known that we were giving tours up in the light, we'd have so many people we couldn't handle. They'd come out in droves.*

*There used to be a wooden structure on top of the fire tower. A pretty good windstorm tore pieces of the roof off and we found them on station property. We figured this would become a real hazard; that the structure itself could blow off the top of the tower. So we got permission to remove it around 1972-73. The tower itself was totally empty when I got there. We kept it closed up.*

Officer Conant and his men installed paneling on the walls and heat in the attic. Since he had four children, the second floor bedrooms did not provide sufficient space. He recalled humorous encounters with fishermen who liked casting their lines below the lighthouse property:

*My first experience with surfcasting was at Montauk and with fishermen fighting for position. Sometimes, we'd sit up top and watched the fights. Did they fight? Oh my Lord, yes! If they were standing on a rock and they caught a fish and stepped off that rock to do something, someone else would step on that rock because it was a better place than they had before and they'd get into it good!*

*Most of the guys fished and we had a great time. When we fished we always carried a set of side cutters, a bottle of mercurochrome and band aids because we cut a lot of hooks out of people.*[247]

At the time of automation, Montauk was one of only twelve light stations in the United States still being operated by resident keepers.

On May 23, 1987 a museum opened to the public in the keeper's quarters. Run by the Montauk Historical Society, the museum keeps alive the vibrant and exciting past of this famous historic site through photographs, documents, letters, and a variety of other interesting artifacts, including several Fresnel lenses. Newly added in 2009 was the document for the purchase of Turtle Hill for lighthouse construction by the federal government, signed by President George Washington on January 4, 1796. Cost for the land? $250.

On January 30, 1996 the lighthouse station was equipped with the Coast Guard Differential Global Positioning System (DGPS), which is a radio navigation system that receives GPS positioning information, calculates real-time corrections to that information, and transmits them over select marine radiobeacon transmitters. DGPS provides accuracy within 10-meters (or 32.8-feet), while GPS accuracy is 100-meters (328-feet).

Elsewhere on Montauk, in 1954 the Third District commander decided to close down the Coast Guard stations at Ditch Plains and at Napeague (just west of Montauk) and consolidate their operations with one station on Star Island in Lake Montauk to be called Station Montauk. However, instead of building a new structure on the island, it was decided to transfer the existing historic building at the old Napeague station.

A station first existed at Napeague about 1855 and was replaced with a new one in 1888. It remained active until after World War II, disappearing from the active list by 1948. It was listed as being about ten miles west of Montauk Lighthouse.

The adventurous operation of transferring the station building, which involved the use of a barge, was accomplished by Carl Darenberg (1925-2009). Employed at the time by Davis Brothers House Movers in Patchogue, Long Island, Darenberg proposed to tow the station to its new site, using his personal fishing boat, the *Lynn*.

Dan Rattiner, publisher of *Dan's Papers*, explained, in humorous fashion, how the plan came to be:

> *Darenberg described the work he had done in the Navy during the war and all of the ships that he had transported, without incident, back and forth between Florida and Montauk on the inland waterway. The officials of the Coast Guard said, well he works for Davis Brothers Movers and they must know what they are doing, and they approved it.*
>
> *Back at Davis Brothers, Carl spoke to the management there, explained his plan, said the Coast Guard was enthusiastic about it and the managers…said, well if the United States Coast Guard thinks it's a good idea, then it probably is.*[248]

It must have been quite a scene during 1954 when the Napeague structure was lifted from its foundation and towed across the Montauk Highway and the Long Island Railroad tracks to the bay where a barge awaited. The operation took six months, since the station was blown onto a sandbar during a storm while en route from Napeague Bay. After two months of efforts by tugs to free it, the structure carefully was maneuvered through the inlet at Montauk Harbor and arrived at Star Island. Carl's son, Carl, Jr. recalled at his father's death in December 2009, "Mom was on the inlet with a light shining, trying to tell him where the inlet was. It was snowing and when they went to slow the boat down, the wind was pushing it faster than he could tow it. They had to slow the boat down to get the barge through the inlet."[249]

Kenny Allen and Bruce Beaudreau are seen scraping and painting the tower in 1957. That's the keeper's dwelling at right. (Ira Lewis Collection, Montauk Point Lighthouse Museum)

The author visits Montauk Point Light Station, August 17, 1957. The lighthouse was being painted at the time, with ropes visible to the right of the tower. (Author photo)

It took more than a year before the building was placed on its new foundation and additional construction was completed. Finally, on October 1, 1955 Coast Guard Station Montauk was officially commissioned as an active unit of Group Moriches, which also included stations at Shinnecock (at Hampton Bays) and Moriches (East Moriches).

In addition to search and rescue work, in the late 1970s the emphasis shifted to law enforcement with regular patrols being part of the station's mission since 1978. All boat crews received small arms training with police departments from New York City and Nassau County. Beginning in the 1980s, the station had an anti-drug smuggling unit as part of their operation.

The station remains busy today. On September 30, 2005 the unaccompanied personnel housing at Station Montauk was dedicated to the memory of Petty Officer 3rd Class, Nathan B. Bruckenthal, killed off the coast of Iraq. He was the only Coast Guardsman killed in action since the Vietnam War. The station underwent a massive facelift during 2007-2008 when the administration and garage buildings were gutted and rebuilt and new construction was completed.

In 2006, Sector Long Island Sound (LIS) at New Haven, Connecticut, was established. It involved the merger of Group Moriches and Group/MSO New Haven. Group Moriches became Sector Field Office (SFO) Moriches and today falls under Sector LIS as a logistical detachment, no longer handling search and rescue/law enforcement cases and no longer a separate command. All members of SFO Moriches conduct regular visits to outlying units as part of their daily routine to assist in handling problems that may occur. They also assist in preparing units for inspections as well as numerous other responsibilities. Station Montauk is a part of Sector LIS.

In 1967 U. S. Coast Guard operations were transferred to the Department of Transportation. Then in 2003, given the circumstances following the attack of "9-11", the Coast Guard was transferred to the Department of Homeland Security. Today, more than ever, the protection of our country's borders has become of vital importance. Station Montauk is a proud contributor to that responsibility.

Mounted on a barge, the Napeague Coast Guard Station is seen on its way to its new location on Star Island in Lake Montauk, 1954. (Courtesy of the East Hampton Library, Long Island Collection)

Napeague Coast Guard Station is pictured at the inlet to Lake Montauk, undergoing relocation in March 1955. The odyssey took about six months to complete. (Courtesy of the East Hampton Library, Long Island Collection)

# Conclusion

WITH THE DEVELOPMENT of sophisticated satellite technology, the need for military coastal defense operations on Montauk became obsolete. By virtue of its geography and proximity to the cities of New York, Boston, and others, the once lonely peninsula of the days of the Montaukett Indians changed with the needs of the times. Where once arrows flew and muskets boomed, eventually came modern, sophisticated weaponry capable of rendering mass destruction. At Camp Hero alone could be seen numerous changes and additions to existing radar systems until they, too, became dinosaurs. From the days when Montauk was a place where few dared tread, it became a lively military town where weapons of land, sea, and air combined to protect the citizens of the northeast from enemy intrusion. And then, having served its purpose, Montauk, with its patriotic, proud citizens, ended its service to its country. Today, the town is still lively, with some four thousand year-round residents, and in-season tourists that swell the population fourfold. However, one can still find places to enjoy the scenery and solitude.

Amid the beauty and mystery that is Montauk lies an alluring history that is truly unlike any other community on Long Island, and probably holds a unique place in American history as well. We do well to remember that this beautiful, pristine peninsula was once an integral part of our country's coastal defense systems—an American Gibraltar.

# Bibliography

## Books and Articles

Bailey, Paul. *Long Island: A History of Two Great Counties; Nassau and Suffolk*. New York: Lewis Publishing Co., Inc., 1949.

*East Hampton Trustees Journal*. Town of East Hampton, 1926, 1927. Volumes 1772-1807, 1807-1826, 1897-1925.

Gardiner David. "Chronicles of the Town of Easthampton, County of Suffolk, New York." *Exploring the Past: Writings from 1798 to 1896 Relating to the Town of East Hampton*, ed. Tom Twomey, pp. 105 – 226.

Gardiner, John Lyon. "Notes and Observations on the Town of East Hampton at the End of Long Island." *Exploring the Past: Writings from 1798 to 1896 Relating to the Town of East Hampton*, ed. Tom Twomey, pp. 1–39. New York: Newmarket Press, 2000.

Geus, Averill Dayton. *From Sea to Sea: 350 Years of East Hampton History*. West Kennebunk, ME: Phoenix Publishing, 1999.

Guernsey, Rocellus Sheridan. *New York and Vicinity during the War of 1812*. Volume II. New York: Charles L. Woodward, Bookseller, 1895.

Hazelton, Henry Isham. *The Boroughs of Brooklyn and Queens, Counties of Nassau and Suffolk*. Volume I. New York: Lewis Historical Publishing Co., 1925.

Heatley, Jeff. *Bully! Colonel Theodore Roosevelt, The Rough Riders and Camp Wikoff*. Montauk Historical Society: Pushcart Press, 1998.

Heatley, Jeff. "Col. Theodore Roosevelt, The Rough Riders and Camp Wikoff." *Awakening the Past: The East Hampton 350th Anniversary Lecture Series 1998*, ed. Tom Twomey, pp. 391-406. New York: Newmarket Press, 1999.

Hedges, Henry. *History of the Town of East Hampton, N. Y.* Sag Harbor: J. H. Hunt, 1897.

Hefner, Robert. "History of East Hampton." easthamptonvillage.org.

*Journals of the Proceedings of the Provincial Congress, Provincial Convention, Committee of Safety and Council of the State of New York*. Albany: Thurlow Weed & Co., 1842.

Manley, Seon. *Long Island Discovery*. Garden City: Doubleday, 1966.

McKinley, William. *Speeches and Addresses of William McKinley*. New York: Doubleday & McClure Co., 1900.

Osmers, Henry. *Living on the Edge: Life at the Montauk Point Lighthouse 1930-1945*. Denver: Outskirts Press, 2009.

_____, _____. *On Eagle's Beak: A History of the Montauk Point Lighthouse*. Denver: Outskirts Press, 2008.

Pelletreau, William S. "East Hampton." *Exploring the Past: Writings from 1798 to 1896 Relating to the History of the Town of East Hampton*, ed. Tom Twomey. New York: Newmarket Press, 2000.

_____, _____. *A History of Long Island; From its Earliest Settlement to the Present Time,* Volume II. New York: Lewis Publishing Co, 1905.

Rattray, Everett. *The South Fork: The Land and the People of Eastern Long Island*. Wainscott: Pushcart Press, 1989.

Rattray, Jeannette Edwards. *East Hampton History*. Garden City: Country Life Press, 1953.

_____, _____. *Montauk: Three Centuries of Romance, Sport and Adventure*. East Hampton: The Star Press, 1938.

_____, _____. *Ship Ashore!* New York: Coward-McCann, Inc., 1955.

Strong, John A. *The Montaukett Indians of Eastern Long Island*. Syracuse: Syracuse University Press, 2001.

Taylor, Theodore. *The Magnificent Mitscher*. Annapolis: Naval Institute Press, 1954.

Thompson, Benjamin F. *The History of Long Island*. 2nd edition. New York: Gould, Banks & Co., 1843.

Toland, John. *The Great Dirigibles: Their Triumphs and Disasters*. New York: Dover Publications, 1972.

Tooker, William Wallace. *Indian Place Names on Long Island*. New York: G. P. Putnam's Sons, 1911.

Twomey, Tom ed. *Awakening the Past: The East Hampton 350th Anniversary Lecture Series 1998*. New York: Newmarket Press, 1999.

_____, _____. *Discovering the Past: Writings of Jeannette Edwards Rattray 1895-1974*. New York: Newmarket Press, 2001.

_____, _____. *Exploring the Past: Writings from 1798 to 1896 Relating to the History of the Town of East Hampton*. New York: Newmarket Press, 2000.

_____, _____. *Tracing the Past: The Writings of Henry P. Hedges 1817 – 1911*. New York: Newmarket Press, 2000.

Winski, Peg. *Montauk: An Anecdotal History*. Montauk Historical Society, 1997.

Wood, Silas. "Excerpts from a Sketch of the First Settlement of the Several Towns on Long Island, with Their Political Condition to the End of the American Revolution." *Exploring the Past: Writings from 1798 to 1896 Relating to the Town of East Hampton*, ed. Tom Twomey, pp. 73 – 93.

## Newspapers, Magazines and Newsletters

*The Beacon*. Montauk Historical Society. 2002 edition.

*Brooklyn Daily Eagle*

*Dan's Papers*

*East Hampton Star*

*Long Island Forum,* July 1981

*The Long Islander*

*Long Island Historical Journal*, July 1938

*Montauk Pioneer*

*National Republic,* June 1944

*New York Herald*
*New York Times*
*Port Jefferson Echo*
*Sag Harbor Express*
*Suffolk County News*
*The Sun*
*The World*
*Time,* August 5, 1929.
*Time,* August 24, 1931.


## Other Sources

Edwards, Thomas. "Reminiscences of Old East Hampton by the Sea." 1929.
Hefner, Robert. Montauk Point Light Station, Montauk, New York. Keeper's Dwelling; A Historic Structures
    Report, October, 1988.
The History Project (East Hampton). East Hampton Library, 1999.
National Archives, Washington, D.C.


## Author's Interviews

Alice Cullen
Ralph W. (Bill) Conant
Frank (Shank) Dickinson
Arthur (Art) Dunne
John Ecker
Vincent (Vinnie) Grimes
Winford Gronley
Fred Houseknecht
Philip Lewis
Byron Lindsey
Bruce McAuliffe
Milton Miller
Frank Tuma
Dave Webb
Richard (Dick) White

# Endnotes

## Chapter 1 – Montaukett Indians

1 Averill Dayton Geus, *From Sea to Sea: 350 Years of East Hampton History* (West Kennebunk, ME: Phoenix Publishing, 1999), 3.

2 William Wallace Tooker, *The Indian Place Names on Long Island and Islands Adjacent* (New York: G. P. Putnam's Sons, 1911), 141-142.

3 Jeannette Edwards Rattray, *East Hampton History* (Garden City: Country Life Press, 1953), 22.

4 John Lyon Gardiner, "Notes and Observations on the Town of East Hampton at the End of Long Island", in *Exploring the Past: Writings from 1798 to 1896 Relating to the Town of East Hampton,* ed. Tom Twomey (New York: Newmarket Press, 2000), 26.

5 Silas Wood, "Excerpts from a Sketch of the First Settlement of the Several Towns on Long Island, with Their Political Condition to the End of the American Revolution", in *Exploring the Past: Writings from 1798 to 1896 Relating to the Town of East Hampton,* ed. Tom Twomey (New York: Newmarket Press, 2000), 79-80.

6 David Gardiner, "Chronicles of the Town of Easthampton, County of Suffolk, New York", in *Exploring the Past: Writings from 1798 to 1896 Relating to the Town of East Hampton,* ed. Tom Twomey (New York: Newmarket Press, 2000), 143.

7 David Gardiner, 144.

8 Tooker, 294-295.

9 Richard F. White interview, March 25, 2010.

10 Seon Manley, *Long Island Discovery* (Garden City: Doubleday, 1966), 30.

11 John A. Strong, *The Montaukett Indians of Eastern Long Island* (Syracuse: Syracuse University Press, 2001), 27.

12 Robert Hefner. "History of East Hampton." www.easthamptonvillage.org .

13 Strong, 30.

14 Benjamin F. Thompson, *The History of Long Island.* 2nd edition (New York: Gould, Banks & Co., 1843), 298.

## Chapter 2 – American Revolution

15 *Journals of the Proceedings of the Provincial Congress, Provincial Convention, Committee of the*

Safety and Council of the State of New York (hereinafter referred to as Proc. Prov. Cong), (Albany: Thurlow Weed & Co., 1842), I, 35.

16 Everett Rattray, The South Fork: The Land and the People of Eastern Long Island (Wainscott: Pushcart Press, 1989), 76.

17 East Hampton Trustees Journal 1772-1807. Town of East Hampton, 1936, 90.

18 Proc. Prov. Cong. I, 110.

19 William S. Pelletreau, "East Hampton", in Exploring the Past: Writings from 1798 to 1896 Relating to the History of the Town of East Hampton, ed. Tom Twomey (New York: Newmarket Press, 2000), 373.

20 Proc. Prov. Cong. I, 383.

*Legend says Hulbert's company created a Stars and Stripes flag before that made by Betsy Ross.

21 Tracing the Past: The Writings of Henry P. Hedges 1817-1911, ed. Tom Twomey (New York: Newmarket Press, 2000), 27.

22 Ibid, 26-27.

23 Pelletreau, "East Hampton," 370-371.

24 Jeannette Edwards Rattray, Montauk: Three Centuries of Romance, Sport and Adventure, (East Hampton: The Star Press, 1938), 60-61.

25 Paul Bailey, Long Island: A History of Two Great Counties; Nassau and Suffolk, (New York: Lewis Publishing Co., Inc., 1949), 89.

26 Letter from Henry B. Livingston to George Washington, August 30, 1776. Montauk Library.

27 Geus, 40.

28 Geus, 41.

29 East Hampton Trustees Journal 1772-1807, 95.

30 East Hampton Trustees Journal 1772-1807, 99.

31 East Hampton Trustees Journal 1772-1807, 104.

32 Everett Rattray. 190.

33 William S. Pelletreau, "East Hampton," 375.

34 Jeannette Edwards Rattray, Montauk, 62.

35 Jeannette Edwards Rattray, Montauk, 61.

36 East Hampton Trustees Journal 1772-1807, 17.

## Chapter 3 – The War of 1812

37 East Hampton Trustees Journal 1807-1826, 21.

38 "Old Letters," Sag Harbor Express, August 19, 1886.

39 Jeannette Edwards Rattray, Montauk, 62.

40 Letter from Joseph H. Hand to Nathaniel Huntting, April 3, 1813. Montauk Point Lighthouse Museum.

41 Henry P. Dering to Secretary of Treasury. January 3, 1814. National Archives, Record Group 26. Correspondence of the Light-House Establishment 1785-1852. Superintendent's Correspondence, Sag Harbor.

42 Henry P. Dering to Sec of Treasury. March 2, 1815. National Archives, Record Group 26. Correspondence of the Light-House Establishment 1785-1852. Superintendent's Correspondence, Sag Harbor.

43 Rocellus Sheridan Guernsey. *New York and Vicinity During the War of 1812*, Volume II (New York: Charles L. Woodward, Bookseller, 1895), 194.

44 Guernsey, 194.

45 Jeannette Edwards Rattray. *Montauk, 62.*

46 *East Hampton Trustees Journal 1772-1807, 23.*

47 *East Hampton Trustees Journal 1772-1807, 23.*

48 William S. Pelletreau, *A History of Long Island; From its Earliest Settlement to the Present Time*, Volume II (New York: Lewis Publishing Co, 1905), 487.

49 *East Hampton Trustees Journal 1807-1826.* Town of East Hampton, 1926. 28.

## Chapter 4 — The Civil War

50 Thomas Edwards, "Reminiscences of Old East Hampton by the Sea," 1929. Unpublished. 104.

## Chapter 5 — The Spanish-American War

51 Henry Hedges. *History of the Town of East Hampton, N. Y.,* (Sag Harbor: J. H. Hunt, 1897), 242-243.

52 "At Camp Baldwin, Montauk," *Brooklyn Daily Eagle,* July 25, 1897.

53 "The Weakest Spot in New York's Defenses," *Brooklyn Daily Eagle,* April 10, 1898.

54 "Montauk Army Corps: May be Established by War Department," *Brooklyn Daily Eagle,* June 5, 1898.

55 Geus, 76.

56 Peg Winski, *Montauk: An Anecdotal History* (Montauk Historical Society, 1997), 17.

57 Jeff Heatley, "Col. Theodore Roosevelt, The Rough Riders & Camp Wikoff," in *Awakening the Past: The 350th Anniversary Lecture Series 1998,* Tom Twomey ed. (New York: Newmarket Press, 1999), 396.

58 "Rushing Work at Old Montauk," *New York Herald,* August 8, 1898.

59 "507 Heroes Home From Santiago," *The World* (NY), August 14, 1898.

60 "Watching for the Transports," *Brooklyn Daily Eagle,* August 19, 1898.

61 "Rushing Work at Old Montauk," *New York Herald,* August 8, 1898.

62 "Roosevelt and Wheeler Ashore," *New York Herald,* August 16, 1898.

63 "Roosevelt and Wheeler Ashore.".

64 "Roosevelt Lauds His Men," *The Sun* (NY), August 16, 1898.

65 "Wheeler Praises Roosevelt," *The World* (NY), August 17, 1898.

66 "Proud Fighters in Tented Camps," *The World* (NY), August 18, 1898.

67 Frank Dickinson interview, March 26, 2010.

68 Jeannette Edwards Rattray, *Montauk, 27.*

69 Jeannette Edwards Rattray, *Montauk, 29.*

70 Jeff Heatley, "Col. Theodore Roosevelt," 392.

71 "Death Ship!" *The World* (NY), August 20, 1898.

72 "Death Ship!"

73 "Death Ship!"

74 Salvatore LaGumina, "Camp Wikoff: 'That Accursed Place,'" *Long Island Forum,* July 1981, 146.

75 LaGumina, 148.

76 "Where a Great Army Rests from its Toil," *Brooklyn Daily Eagle,* August 17, 1898.

77 "Sick Land in Surf Boats," *The Sun* (NY), August 27, 1898.

78 "Sick Land in Surf Boats."

79 "Sick Land in Surf Boats."

80 "Caring for 2,140 Sick," *The Sun* (NY), August 29, 1898.

81 "Yellow Fever at Montauk," *New York Times*, August 30, 1899.

82 LaGumina, 149.

83 "Montauk's Great Day," *New York Times*, September 4, 1898.

84 "Montauk's Great Day."

85 "Montauk's Great Day."

86 William McKinley, *Speeches and Addresses of William McKinley* (New York: Doubleday & McClure Co., 1900), 81-82.

87 Jeff Heatley, editor, *Bully! Colonel Theodore Roosevelt, The Rough Riders and Camp Wikoff* (Montauk Historical Society: Pushcart Press, 1998), 247.

88 "Remember Camp Wikoff," *East Hampton Star*, September 9, 1898.

89 Charles Johnson Post, "Montauk: A Chronicle of '98," *Long Island Historical Journal*, July 1938.

90 Post.

91 "Montauk Point Light," *The Sun* (NY), September 7, 1898.

92 Henry Osmers, *On Eagle's Beak: A History of the Montauk Point Lighthouse* (Denver: Outskirts Press, 2008), 91-93.

93 "Rough Riders Their Heroes," *Brooklyn Daily Eagle,* August 26, 1898.

94 Manley, 247.

95 "Roosevelt's Farewell," *The Sun* (NY), September 14, 1898.

96 "Roosevelt to War Board," *New York Times*, November 23, 1898.

97 Henry Isham Hazelton, *The Boroughs of Brooklyn and Queens, Counties of Nassau and Suffolk.* Volume I(New York: Lewis Historical Publishing Co., 1925), 295.

98 "Report of the War Commission," *New York Times*, February 13, 1899.

99 "Popular Negro Soldiers," *The Sun* (NY), August 29, 1898.

100 "Roosevelt's Farewell," *The Sun* (NY), September 14, 1898.

101 Everett Rattray, 129.

102 Everett Rattray, 139.

103 "Life Saving Stations," *Sag Harbor Express*, October 20, 1898.

104 "Montauk Attacked by Naval Enemy," *Brooklyn Daily Eagle*, September 4, 1902.

# Chapter 6 – World War I

105 "Nine Days of Toil for State Cavalry," *New York Times,* June 16, 1913.

106 *East Hampton Trustees Journal 1897-1925*. Town of East Hampton, 1927. 322.

107 *East Hampton Trustees Journal 1897-1925*, 324.

108 "Island News Notes," *Suffolk County News*, April 16, 1915.

109 "No Submarines Seen off Montauk Point," *New York Times*, March 30, 1917.

110 "U.S. Navy Third Naval District, Section 4 Memoirs, Montauk." January 1, 1919. Pamphlet.

111 Winski, 49.

112 Hazelton, 571.

113 Hazelton, 531.

114 "Aviation Camp at Montauk, "*East Hampton Star,* August 24, 1917.

115 "Aviation Camp at Montauk.".

116 Theodore Taylor, *The Magnificent Mitscher* (Annapolis: Naval Institute Press, 1954), 46.

117 Taylor, 46.

118 "Montauk's First Naval Air Station," Carlos C. Hanks. *National Republic.* June, 1944.

119 "Boys at Montauk want Comforts," *East Hampton Star,* September 28, 1917.

120 "U.S. Navy Third Naval District, Section 4 Memoirs, Montauk." January 1, 1919. Pamphlet

121 "Montauk's First Naval Air Station." Carlos C. Hanks. *National Republic.* June, 1944.

122 "Military Dance," *East Hampton Star,* February 15, 1918.

123 "Montauk Air Station Notes," *East Hampton Star,* May 31, 1918.

124 "Base No. 5 Leads League," *Suffolk County News,* July 12, 1918.

125 Robert Hefner, "Montauk Point Light Station Keeper's Dwelling; A Historic Structures Report, October, 1988, 210.

126 "Y.M.C.A. Hut Opened at Montauk Naval Base, "*East Hampton Star,* September 13, 1918.

127 "Montauk to Paris," *Montauk Pioneer,* April 26, 2002. Dan Rattiner.

128 "C-4, Biggest Dirigible in U. S. Makes Successful Flight," *East Hampton Star,* February 14, 1919.

129 John Toland, The *Great Dirigibles: Their Triumphs and Disasters* (New York: Dover Publications, 1972), 58.

130 "To Dismantle Montauk Camp," *East Hampton Star,* December 26, 1919.

131 "Gay Gobs at Montauk," *New York Times,* November 16, 1919.

132 "Gay Gobs at Montauk."

133 "Easy Life at Montauk Camp," *East Hampton Star,* January 30, 1920.

134 "Dismantle Hangar," *East Hampton Star,* March 19, 1920.

135 "Bomb House Torn Down in 3 Days," *East Hampton Star,* May 21, 1920.

136 "Great Activity at Fort Pond," *East Hampton Star,* August 13, 1920.

## Chapter 7 – Camp Welsh

137 "Guns Boom at Montauk," *Port Jefferson Echo,* July 2, 1921.

138 "May Not Have Montauk Camp," *East Hampton Star,* February 24, 1922.

139 "Montauk Point Camp Site," *East Hampton Star,* April 21, 1922.

140 "Montauk Camp Site Surveyed," *East Hampton Star,* May 12, 1922.

141 "1800 Regulars at Camp Welsh," *East Hampton Star,* August 11, 1922.

142 "1800 Regulars at Camp Welsh."

143 "Island News Notes," *Suffolk County News,* January 20, 1922.

144 "Island News Notes," *Suffolk County News,* October 20 1922.

145 "Troops Leave Road in Bad Shape," *Port Jefferson Echo,* October 14, 1922.

146 "Many Robberies at Camp Welsh.," *East Hampton Star*, August 25, 1922.

147 "Gun Practice at Camp Welsh," *East Hampton Star,* August 25, 1922.

138 Richard F. White interview, March 25, 2010.

139 "Britton Pushes Montauk Naval Base Proposal," *Port Jefferson Echo,* January 20, 1931.

150 "Montauk Maneuver," *Time,* August 24, 1931.

151 "Montauk Maneuver."

152 "Montauk Maneuver."

153 "Montauk Maneuver."

154 "Praises Montauk as Fleet Departs," *New York Times,* August 18, 1931.

## Chapter 8 – World War II

155 "Plan 4 New Air Bases," *New York Times,* January 28, 1940.

156 "Fair to Dramatize Coast Guard Work," *New York Times,* March 31, 1940.

157 Robert and Miriam Byrnes interview, April 11, 1998. The History Project (East Hampton).

158 Dan Rattiner. "The Village That Isn't There," *Dan's Papers,* November 21, 2003.

159 Everett Rattray, 129.

160 Dan Rattiner. "The Village That Isn't There," *Dan's Papers,* November 21, 2003.

161 Winski, 47.

162 "Restrictions on Commercial Use of Fort Pond Bay," *East Hampton Star,* May 6, 1943.

163 "'Tin Fish' for Planes and Subs Get Final O. K. at Montauk Range before Attack on Enemy," *East Hampton Star,* February 24, 1944.

164 Winski, 50.

165 Winski, 69-70.

166 Vinnie Grimes interview, October 2, 2009.

167 "Montauk USO to Give Awards for Hostess' Work," *East Hampton Star,* October 19, 1944.

168 "Montauk USO Closes After 16 Months of Service," *East Hampton Star,* March 8, 1945.

169 "Navy Buildings at Montauk Base Offered for Sale, *East Hampton Star,* April 19, 1945.

170 National Archives, Record Group 26. Lighthouse Station logs 1897-1946. Box 107.

171 "Montauk," *East Hampton Star,* January 15, 1942.

172 Hefner, 87, 97.

173 Henry Osmers, *Living on the Edge: Life at the Montauk Point Lighthouse 1930-1945* (Denver: Outskirts Press, 2008), 91.

174 Osmers, 93.

175 Jack Graves. "A Man Who Changed Collars." *East Hampton Star.* June 23, 1977.

176 Kurt Kahofer. "Fire Control Station," *The Beacon,* Montauk Historical Society. Summer 2002.

177 "Army Takes Montauk 468-Acre Site," *The Long Islander,* January 22, 1942.

178 "National Affairs: Admiral vs. General," *Time,* August 5, 1929.

179 "Montauk's Old Mill Moves Again," *New York Times,* August 16, 1942.

180 Carl Dordelman interview, January 27, 1999. The History Project (East Hampton), 1999.

181 Frank Tuma interview, March 26, 2010.

182 "Long Island's Eastern Shield." Headquarters First US Army. Governor's Island, New York. January 14, 1958. Report.

183 Everett Rattray, 119.

184 Frank Dickinson interview, March 26, 2010.

185 "Long Island's Eastern Shield."

186 Dave Webb interview, March 26, 2010.

187 Winski, 63.

188 Milton Miller interview, August 13, 2010.

189 Richard F. White interview, March 25, 2010.

190 "Long Island's Eastern Shield."

191 "Architectural Documentation and Recordation of the Ditch Plains Artillery Fire Control Stations in the Bear & Schub Subdivision, Montauk, Town of East Hampton, Suffolk County, New York." June 1998. Report.

192 "Fortress Hamptons," *Dan's Papers,* June 11, 2004.

193 Adele Cramer. "Ditch Plains Artillery Fire Control Stations: A report." March 1995.

194 "Fortress Hamptons," *Dan's Papers,* June 11, 2004.

195 Everett Rattray, 119.

196 "Montauk 1960: A Long Look at the Point's Past, Present- and Future," *East Hampton Star,* May 26, 1960.

197 "Montauk 1960: A Long Look at the Point's Past, Present- and Future."

198 Vinnie Grimes interview, October 2, 2009.

199 Transcript of interviews with Montauk residents on Major Bowes Chrysler Hour, 1940. Montauk Library.

200 U. S. Army Program Manager for Chemical Demilitarization Survey and Analysis Report, Second Edition. December 1996.

## Chapter 9 – The Cold War Years and Camp Hero 1946-1980s

201 "Guns of Montauk Being Dismantled," *New York Times,* February 6, 1949.

202 Jim Sullivan interview for Montauk Library, March 18, 2003.

203 Janis Hewitt, "Sunday's Grand Marshal," *East Hampton Star,* March 18, 2004.

204 Fred Houseknecht interview, September 18, 2009.

205 Dave Webb interview, March 26, 2010.

*Prior to Camp Hero, a radar site was known to exist atop Prospect Hill off East Lake Drive on Montauk as early as 1942.

206 "No Nike Missiles for Montauk Point," East Hampton Star, August 12, 1965.

207 "First Army Moves to Montauk Plains for Maneuvers," *The Long Islander,* February 8, 1951.

208 Ibid.

209 Richard F. White interview, March 25, 2010.

210 "Army Order Rules Out Montauk Fishing," *The Long Islander,* March 8, 1951.

211 "Boats Warned Fort Hero Anti-aircraft Practice Resumes off Point Monday," *East Hampton Star,* January 3, 1952.

212 "Army Resumes Firing off Montauk Mon., Feb. 4." *East Hampton Star,* January 31, 1952.

213 Russell Drumm, "Rally Round the Radar, " *East Hampton Star,* December 23, 1999.

214 Carl Dordelman interview, January 27, 1999. The History Project (East Hampton), 1999.

215 Winford Gronley interview, June 4, 2010.

216 Jim Sullivan interview for Montauk Library, March 18, 2003.

217 Jim Sullivan interview for Montauk Library, March 18, 2003.

218 Bill Bleyer, "The Russians Were Coming," *Newsday,* March 10, 2002.

219 Jim Sullivan interview for Montauk Library, March 18, 2003.

220 Jim Sullivan interview for Montauk Library, March 18, 2003.

221 Richard F. White interview, March 25, 2010.

222 Vinnie Grimes interview, October 2, 2009.

223 Richard F. White interview, March 25, 2010.

224 "No Nike Missiles for Montauk Point," *East Hampton Star,* August 12, 1965.

225 "The Montauk Air Force Station," *East Hampton Star,* February 23, 1967.

226 Bruce McAuliffe interview, June 4, 2010,

227 Byron Lindsey interview, June 18, 2010.

228 Letter from Town of East Hampton to Airmen, December 4, 1974. Montauk Library.

229 Ralph W. Conant interview, August 8, 2010.

230 "Seamy Side of the USAF," *East Hampton Star,* October 16, 1975.

231 "Seamy Side of the USAF."

232 "Radar Base is Mourned," *East Hampton Star,* May 4, 1978.

233 "Radar Base is Mourned."

234 Frances Cerra, "Montauk: Last Outpost of a Military Era," *New York Times,* May 21, 1978.

235 John Hanc, "Montauk's Unsung Hero," *Newsday,* June 26, 2003.

## Chapter 10 – The United States Coast Guard

236 "Station Montauk Point," www.uscg.mil/history/stations/MontaukPoint.pdf.

237 Jeannette Edwards Rattray, *Ship Ashore!* (New York: Coward, McCann, Inc., 1955), 92.

238 Richard F. White interview, March 25, 2010.

239 John Ecker interview, March 26, 2010.

240 Milton Miller interview, August 13, 2010.

241 "U.S. Coast Guard Oral History Program; Interview with John C.Cullen," March 30, 2006. www.uscg.mil/history/weboralhistory/CullenJohn03302006.pdf

242 Alice Cullen interview, April 23, 2010.

243 *United States Coast Guard Book of Valor* (Washington D.C.: Public Relations Division, May 1945)

244 Alice Cullen interview, April 23, 2010.

245 Letters to the Editor, *East Hampton Star*, September 2, 2010.

246 Philip Lewis interview, February 8, 2010.

247 Ralph W. Conant interview, August 8, 2010.

248 Dan Rattiner, "House on the Move," *Montauk Pioneer,* May 10, 2002.

249 Mitchell Freedman, "LI Marina Owner, Boat Captain Carl Darenberg Sr. dies," *Newsday,* December 29, 2009.

# Index

# ALSO BY Henry Osmers

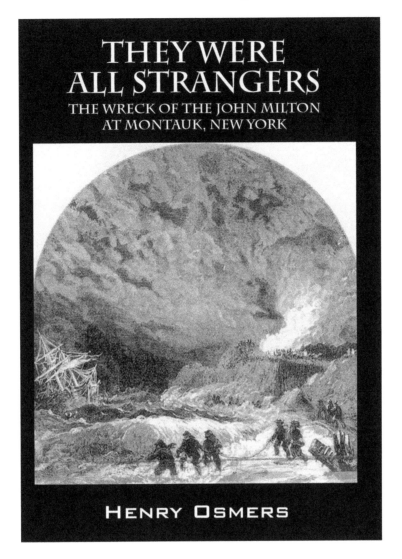

## *They Were All Strangers*

"'They Were All Strangers' captures the dismal drama of a nineteenth century shipwreck - the heartbreak, horror, and sometimes lurid fascination. Henry Osmers' meticulous research and penchant for good storytelling has produced yet another excellent tale of Long Island maritime history."

—Elinor DeWire, Author "Guardians of the Lights"

**Learn more at: www.outskirtspress.com/theywereallstrangers**

CPSIA information can be obtained
at www.ICGtesting.com
Printed in the USA
BVHW011307220921
617302BV00014B/179

9 781432 774387